Why LOVE Doesn't Last

BY
SHEILA WHALUM

WHY LOVE DOESN'T LAST
Sheila Whalum

This book or parts thereof may not be reproduced in any form, stored in a retrieval system, or transmitted in any form by any means—electronic, mechanical, photocopy, recording or otherwise—without prior written permission of the publisher, author or legal representative of both or either parties, except as provided by United States of America copyright law.

Copyright © 2014 by Sheila Whalum

Published by Pecan Tree Publishing, October 2014
Hollywood, FL
www.pecantreebooks.com

Library of Congress Control Number: 2014954174
ISBN: 978-0-9888969-5-6

PECAN TREE PUBLISHING
Hollywood, Fl.
www.pecantreepress.com

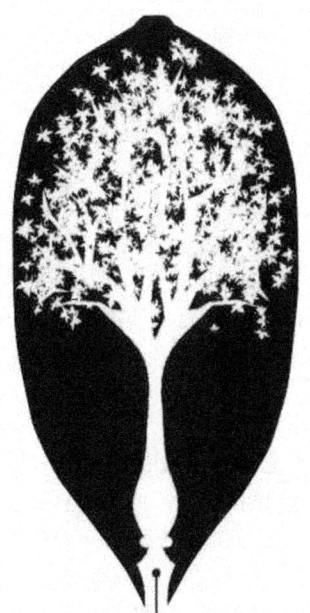

New Voices | New Styles | New Vision

WHY LOVE DOESN'T LAST

Creative Director
Kenneth Whalum III

Image Advisor
Kortland Whalum

Marketing Director
Kameron Whalum

Front and Back Cover Design
Andrew Thiele
arteknyc.com

Printing
Pecan Tree Publishing

Book Cover Photo
My first train ride to the Bronx in New York
Gregory L. Morgan Jr.
http://jshotti.com

Contributing Editors
Dr. Kenneth T. Whalum, Jr.
Emily Claudette Freeman

Endorsements
Marcie Cleary
Tracy Bethea
Dr. Kenneth T. Whalum, Jr.

ACKNOWLEDGMENTS

To the Man who treats me (Sheila Ann Lee Whalum)
like a Queen, STILL after 32 years:
Dr. Kenneth T. Whalum, Jr.

To my three talented sons:
Kenneth T. Whalum III
Kortland Kirk Whalum
Kameron Timothy Whalum

To my beautiful daughter-in-law
Crystal Whalum (Kenneth) and my first grandson, Kenneth T. Whalum IV

In memory of some amazing and special women in my life:
My Mother, Margaret White Lee
My younger sister and biggest fan, Angela Ladale Lee Farmer
Dr. Loretta Bobo Mosley

In honor of my Mother-in-Law,
Mary Helen Whalum Rogers (Ormer)

To my Dad,
Willie Peter Lee (Mel)

To my siblings:
Kenneth A. Lee
Wanda Lee-Howell
Margaret Jackson

To the White, Lee & Whalum Families

To the Pleasant Grove Baptist Church, Sunset, Arkansas

To the C.A.N.A. Married Couples' Class of The New Olivet Baptist
Church Memphis, Tennessee

Acknowledgments

To The New Olivet Baptist Church Family

I LOVE YOU!

To FOX 13 and the entire Good Morning Memphis Crew!
Thanks for making me feel so special on Tuesdays and calling me "The Relationship Expert." It has been the best time of my life. You gave me an opportunity to show real love in a real marriage and offer help to marriages all across Memphis and the surrounding areas. Many in your viewing audience watched Couples Achieving Newness Again (C.A.N.A.) and reached out to me letting me know they appreciate the marriage/relationship tips.

FOREWORD

The Author, The Relationship Expert, The Woman
By
Mrs. Vanessa Peterson

Sheila Whalum possesses an uncanny innate ability to reign wherever her delicate, but deliberate footsteps land. Her reign as a chosen woman of God is seen in her familial relationships, where she is the proud wife of Dr. Kenneth T. Whalum, Jr. She is the mother of three sons and a daughter-in-law: Kenneth, Kortland, Kameron, and Crystal. In addition, she has one grandson, Kenneth T. Whalum IV. She reigned in City Hall as the Deputy Director of Finance; and she reigns in the world of Education with a Master of Business Administration from the University of Phoenix and a Bachelor of Arts Degree in Communication from the University of Memphis.

She reigns in business as the owner of Christ-Like Modeling and O'Sheilas Beauty and Barber Shop.

This natural power reign is traced back through the roots of royal African American Women. When one considers Sheila's supernatural warrior spirit, we are reminded of Amina, the Queen of Zaria, who at the age of 16 became Queen of her City and battled with others daily, using her fearless military skills and her keen decisiveness.

Sheila's reign is possibly gleaned from Candace, Empress of Ethiopia who's tactical and field commander skills frightened Alexander to the point of halting his army in raging battle to avoid her territory at all costs.

Mrs. Whalum's keen sense of love and loyalty and commitment to her husband is connected to Nefertari, Queen of "Kemet" whose marriage to the great Rameses II is known throughout history as the greatest royal love affair. Monuments remain today as a reminder of their undaunted and untainted love. Mrs. Whalum's subtle, but powerful spirit of activism and refusal to join in any apathetic movement dates back to the reign of Nefertari; who consistently played an active role in the reshaping of a civilization alongside her husband. Together, as one powerful and purposeful entity, they created a new city during their reign.

Mrs. Whalum's fearlessness and ability to necessitate a movement can only be parallel to Queen Yaa Asantewaa of the Asante Empire- who in the middle of a secret meeting of the chiefs stood and stated; *"Now I have seen that some of you feared to go forward to fight for our king. If it were in the brave days of the old, the chiefs would not sit down to see their king taken away without firing a shot."* She and the other leaders fought this battle and this was the last war of the major wars in Africa led by women.

Finally, where does the unmistakable, flawless and impeccable beauty and virtue of Mrs. Sheila Whalum, come from? Well, from the Queen of Sheba, of course-Makeda. She was legendary for her beauty and power. She was always on a journey to find more wisdom and more truth. Likewise, with our very own Queen, Mrs. Sheila Whalum, her King heavily pursued Queen Makeda until she finally gave in to the wooing and the wowing. Therefore, as you pull wisdom from the words in this book you hold in your hands, know that you are gaining lived and learned experience. This is not history from a Lady in Waiting; not from a Princess; nor from a Duchess; but from a great Queen who prevails from a lineage of prominent women and who has experienced love in all its glory and challenges.

CONTENTS

INTRODUCTION xiii

One: Why Men Cheat 1

Two: Are You Stuck In Your Marriage? 4

Three: Where Is The Ring? 7

Four: Love, Sex Or Money 9

Five: Are You Keeping Up With Social Media In Your Marriage? 11

Six: How Happy Are You In Your Marriage? 13

Seven: Is Jealousy Holding Your Marriage Back? 15

Eight: In Marriage You Must Communicate The Right Way 18

Nine: Can Traveling With Your Spouse Enhance Your Marriage? 20

Ten: Is Parenting Wrecking Your Romance? 22

Eleven: Which Do Husbands Rank First, Sex Or A Home-Cooked Meal? . . . 25

Twelve: How Do You Keep Peace In Your Marriage? 27

Thirteen: Are You Flirting Outside Of Your Marriage? 30

Fourteen: Should I Forgive Or Forget? 33

Fifteen: In Marriage, Can What You Wear To Bed Affect
Your Relationship? 35

Sixteen: Do You TRUST Your Spouse? 37

Seventeen: Does The Silent Treatment Help Or Hurt Your Marriage? . . . 40

Contents

Eighteen: Roaming Eyes In Marriage..................................42

Nineteen: Extreme Measures To Save Your Marriage 44

Twenty: Do Pets Help Or Hurt Your Marriage?......................46

Twenty-one: Why The Need To Hyphenate Your Name?
Is This The New Norm?...49

Twenty-two: Husbands Must Have Five Needs Met By Their Wives ... 52

Twenty-three: Do You Have A Strategy To Stay Married? 55

Twenty-four: Can Sex Therapy Help Your Marriage?...................58

Twenty-five: Is Kissing Still Important In Marriage?..................61

Twenty-six: Do You Know Your Spouse's Love Languages?............63

Twenty-seven: Why Did Elizabeth Taylor Marry Eight Times?..........66

Twenty-eight: Is It My Money Or Our Money?
(Would you marry someone with a bad FICO Score?)...................69

Twenty-nine: The Age Factor In Marriage: Does It Matter?.............71

Thirty: Is Your Marriage Stuck In The Crazy Cycle?....................73

Thirty-one: Is Separation Good Or Bad For Your Marriage?............75

Thirty-two: Do You And Your Spouse Share The Same Religion?.......77

Thirty-three: When Was The Last Time Your Husband Opened
The Car Door For You?...80

Thirty-four: Do You Need A Marriage Counselor?.....................82

Thirty-five: Are Into Public Displays Of Affection (PDA's) For,
Or From Your Spouse?...84

Contents

Thirty-six: Can A Glass Of Wine Enhance Your Marriage? 87

Thirty-seven: Is There A Bully In Your Marriage? 89

Thirty-eight: Over One Thousand Benefits For Just Being Married!. 91

Thirty-nine: In Sickness And In Health 93

Forty: Will Pornography Enhance Or Destroy Your Marriage?. 95

Forty-one: Husbands Often Say To Their Wives,
"You Are Not My Mother!". 97

Forty-two: Can A Body Massage Perform Wonders For
Your Marriage?. 100

Forty-three: Can Having A Best Friend Other Than Your
Spouse Enhance Your Marriage?. 102

Forty-four: Can Saying "I Love You" Instead Of "Love You"
Make A Big Difference In Your Marriage?. 104

Forty-five: Is Your Spouse Your Soul Mate?. 106

Forty-six: Have You Given Your Spouse A Hug Today? 108

Forty-seven: Could Eating At Hooters Possibly Enhance
Your Marriage?. 111

Forty-eight: The Policy Of Joint Agreement Will Enhance
Your Marriage. 113

Forty-nine: To Enhance Your Marriage Or Relationship
STOP Domestic Violence 116

Fifty - Final Chapter: Why L O V E Doesn't Last .118

Epilogue. 127

Bibliography 131

Resources For C.A.N.A. Book Club 132

About The Author. 133

INTRODUCTION

Why Love Doesn't Last will reveal just how **love** gets lost in the shuffle. There are just too many distractions! As I sat at Café Bari SoHo in New York, New York working on the last piece to my book, I watched thousands of people walk by. I watched as lovers strolled by. I could tell many were happy; some were sad; and it was clear that many in movement – although holding hands with their lovers - did not want to be bothered.

Whatever kind of relationship you are in, this book will help you clearly see why the love you think you really need, really doesn't last whether you are married or not.

I got married on June 19, 1982, to Dr. Kenneth T. Whalum, Jr. When I think of my husband Kenneth, I think of a quote by noted historian Robert Caro describing President John Fitzgerald Kennedy: "There's a genius about him." That genius quality attracted me to my husband-to-be.

The day I married Kenneth was the best day of my life. I was twenty-two years young, slim, pretty, vivacious, and very charming. Kenneth had seen me in a photograph a couple of years before we actually met. When he saw me in person, I was singing in the choir at my home church. He says he couldn't resist staring at me. (Read **Destined To Be A Preacher's Wife** for the full story). Our journey as one began the day we married. We were so happy and so in love; that love and happiness prompted the start of our family of three boys. I kept house and Kenneth went to work. All the while, we continued loving each other. We knew that God had joined us together because we were on the same spiritual path.

When our sons grew older, I returned to work and school. Even though managing so many duties was hard, Kenneth helped in every regard.

After, three years of marriage, Kenneth was called to be Pastor of a church in Sunset, Arkansas called Pleasant Grove Baptist Church. I became a "First Lady," another duty that I would have to add to my already substantial list. However, Kenneth continued to help me and call me his Queen. I

Introduction

knew that I could do all that I needed to do because I had the love of this wonderful man.

Ten years later, we left that church and went to Olivet Baptist Church in Memphis, Tennessee. Kenneth became Pastor in 1999. I had even more duties, and had to step up my game, because the church was much larger, and there was even more to do. My husband never told me that I had to do anything, but because of the love that he had shown me, I felt obligated to do my part.

After being at Olivet Baptist Church for several years, I assessed the situation of married couples in the church, and the picture wasn't pretty. Several of the married men flirted with me in church. Many of them had beautiful wives, but it appeared they no longer loved them.

Having the beautiful marriage that I had with Kenneth, and with him being the Pastor of the church, I knew that something had to give. As a young wife who took my vows seriously, I did not want to end up like a lot of the married couples that I saw; married, but not in love. Why be married and not be in love? Why?

In 1999, because of what we observed about marriages at Olivet Baptist Church, Kenneth, and I created a class called C.A.N.A., which is an acronym for Couples Achieving Newness Again. This married couples' class was our effort to save marriages from going into that stale stage where the marriage is just about dead.

We wanted couples to know that their marriages could be strong and healthy, even after many years, but both spouses would have to work at it. Fifteen years later, the class is still going and growing strong. In fact, we celebrated C.A.N.A.'s fifteenth year of existence by traveling as a group (twenty-five couples) to the tropical island of Aruba, "One Happy Island," for a one-week vacation. Kenneth and I are still going strong, with thirty-two years of love in our marriage.

A few years after C.A.N.A.'s inception, we started advertising the class by way of a huge outdoor billboard near the church. Every month, that billboard which was seen by thousands of drivers - featured Kenneth and

Introduction

me in some romantic and fun pose. In 2012, I became, by invitation, part of FOX's "Good Morning Memphis" Show. Bi-weekly on Tuesday's my assignment on air is giving C.A.N.A./Relationship tips to help keep marriages strong and healthy in Memphis and the surrounding areas.

Fifty of the messages shared, are condensed into the following pages. They are purposely chosen to let you know that your marriage can last, once you understand all of the dynamics of love, and your relationship can possibly lead to a healthy marriage. I have used my own experience as well as the experiences of others to help you on your way to a great marriage.

I once saw a television documentary called "The Essence of Marriage," which stated, "Weddings come a dime a dozen but marriage is much more rare and much more precious." I have also heard it said, "Women love so hard while men hardly love." Maybe that's why God says in His word that husbands should love their wives and wives should respect their husbands. However, these days, husbands seem to be lusting more for other women than they do their wives. Witnessing this behavior on the part of their husbands often causes wives to treat their husbands with disrespect.

As you can see, Love is very complex, so let's get started. I know that this book will bless you and help you to have a strong, healthy marriage or a healthy relationship that will possibly lead to marriage with your own definition of LOVE.

XV

One
WHY MEN CHEAT

Yes, women cheat too, but men cheat more! Married men, that is! I published a book in 2011 entitled, ***The Stimulus Package: Why Men Cheat.*** In my research, husbands gave many reasons about why they cheat:

- The power of a woman
- They were somewhat "mothered" by the wife
- Peer pressure from other men
- They needed passionate sex
- The wife had gained weight
- She didn't look like she looked ten years ago
- She didn't respect him
- She cheated on him
- They needed more than one woman in their life
- She wasn't exciting anymore

One: Why Men Cheat

I have a real problem with three of those reasons:

1. The wife had gained weight.
   My question: Have You?

2. She didn't look like she did ten years ago.
   My question: Do You?

3. They needed passionate sex.
   My question: What are you going to do when things slow down for you?

   The wives, (when asked why their husbands cheated on them), said they felt their husbands cheated because:
   They can't help themselves.
   Because of their ego.
   Because of what they see.

Men cheat because they need to feel powerful and most men feel powerful in two ways: in the pockets and in the pants, oftentimes not at the same time. In other words, they cheat because of their **"stimulus package."**

One: Why Men Cheat

Tip #1
...

There is never a good reason to cheat. A cheater needs to curb his/her appetite, because a cheater is often greedy. This leads to being out of order and out of line.

When you cheat, you are *not* living your best life!

Couples, YOU CAN ACHIEVE NEWNESS AGAIN!

Two

ARE YOU STUCK IN YOUR MARRIAGE?

Research shows that most things in life come in three stages. Marriage is no different. Do not become stagnant in your marriage. Let's look at the three stages of marriage (also found in my book, ***The Stimulus Package: Why Men Cheat***). As noted by Dr. and Mrs. Lynwood Davis of *The Torch Leader Daily News*, the three stages of marriage are Endearment, Adjustment, and Commitment.

Stage One: Endearment

The Endearment Stage is very easy and short-lived. In this stage, your marriage is untested. It is really fantasyland because all you think about is each other, romance, and sex. This stage may last four or five years. It varies depending upon the circumstances. As perfect as everything may seem, couples will not remain in this stage. According to the Davis', the word *endearment* means the outward expression, verbally and physically, of affection. Dr. and Mrs. Lynwood Davis believe that couples cannot establish their marriage in this stage.

Stage Two: Adjustment

The Adjustment Stage is the most difficult stage of the three. The word *adjustment* simply means to make light changes to make something fit or function better. It means to adapt to a new environment or condition. In this stage you have been married for a while, and both of you realize things have changed. The adjustment stage is where you will find all of your problems: His fault, her fault, the children, the finances, the job, school; you name it. The Davis', who have a dynamic marriage ministry, state that all marriages enter this stage, but few ever leave it.

That means that couples do not deal with their real problems, and often end up miserable, become cheaters, or end up in divorce court, which is tragic when you consider that with a little work those couples could have gotten to stage three if they had adjusted to each other's needs. If you want to keep and save your marriage, you must realize that it is not a question of whose fault it is. It is a question of, "where do we go from here?" You must adjust to whatever the situation is that you cannot change. The Davis' says it this way, "Fight the problem, and not each other." The lesson here is that if there is a major problem or issue, then the two of you must push to get out of the adjustment stage, and into the third and final stage: Commitment. The sad thing is that, many marriages become stuck in the adjustment stage, and never get to commitment. That is why the divorce rate is so high.

Stage Three: Commitment

In The Commitment Stage, both of you have gotten the adjustments right. You have adjusted your marriage to deal with moods (E.g. PMS and Menopause for her; Manopause and Mid-Life crisis for him). You have adjusted your marriage to the different situations and different circumstances that are sure to come. It means you ENJOY each other's company, and you are committed to the end.

Two: Are You Stuck In Your Marriage?

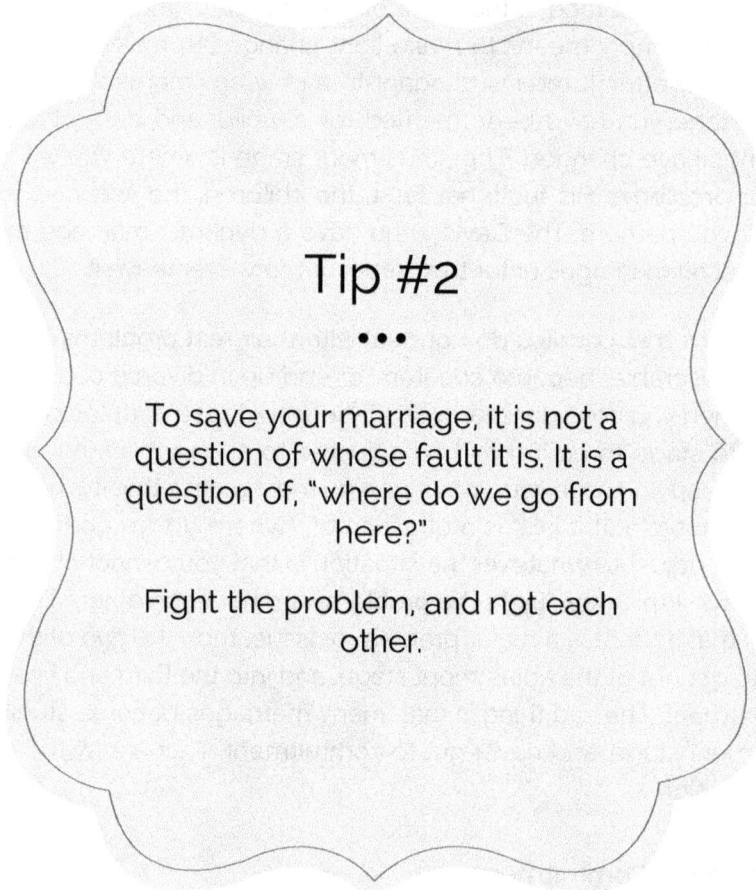

Tip #2

• • •

To save your marriage, it is not a question of whose fault it is. It is a question of, "where do we go from here?"

Fight the problem, and not each other.

Couples, YOU CAN ACHIEVE NEWNESS AGAIN!

Three

WHERE IS THE RING?

You have probably heard, "Where is the beef?" How about - "Where is the ring?" Most marriage ceremonies include a line that says, *"With this ring, I thee wed."* The husband says it as he places the wedding ring on his new wife's finger. Then, the wife says it as she places the wedding ring on her new husband's finger. However, over time, the ring is missing in action, usually from the husband's finger. Various surveys indicate that wives typically wear their wedding rings long-term, while husbands are more likely to stop wearing theirs.

Here are a few reasons given by husbands for not wearing their rings:

1. My wedding band is too small. (Yes, but it's been too small for ten years!)
2. I don't like wearing jewelry.
3. I forgot to put it on. (Really? Give me a break!)
4. My wife knows I love her.

Three: Where Is The Ring?

Tip #3

•••

Couples must agree if either spouse decides *not* to wear the wedding ring.

The ring symbolizes oneness.

Couples, YOU CAN ACHIEVE NEWNESS AGAIN!

Four

WHICH IS BETTER - LOVE, SEX, OR MONEY?

Love is a strong, positive emotion of regard and affection. Most Women *love* to love. When love is not there, they find themselves singing the late Donny Hathaway song "Where is the love you said was mine oh mine 'til the end of time? Was it just a lie? Where is the love?"

Many men have proven that sex is very high on their list of relationship priorities. The desire for sex is so powerful that it drives many decisions that men make, including the decision to commit adultery. Some men take it to the extreme, as proven in a *Wall Street Journal* article a few years ago. The *WSJ* article detailed a recent phenomenon in Japan called, "dating simulation games," in which men interact with female cartoon characters in elaborate situational rendezvous.

In addition, it is difficult to ignore the soaring sales of sexual performance enhancement drugs such as Viagra, Cialis, and others.

The bottom line is that money is certainly great to have. Women see it as security. Men see it as power. At the end of the day, love is better!

Four: Which Is Better - Love, Sex, Or Money?

Tip #4
...

Just simply holding hands sends love through your entire body!

Couples, YOU CAN ACHIEVE NEWNESS AGAIN!

Five

ARE YOU KEEPING UP WITH SOCIAL MEDIA IN YOUR MARRIAGE?

People all over the world are staying "connected" via Facebook, Twitter, Instagram, cell phones, etc.

Wives: If your husband has a Facebook account, a Twitter account, and the latest smart phone technology, which enable him to connect with people all over the world, you should have the same. What's your handle?

If neither spouse is connected, that's great. At least you're together! Often, problems arise when only one spouse is a part of the social media world.

The spouse that is a part of social media should educate the other spouse on the use of this contemporary tool of networking and friendship, just in case they want to get their own social media accounts.

Five: Are You Keeping Up With Social Media In Your Marriage?

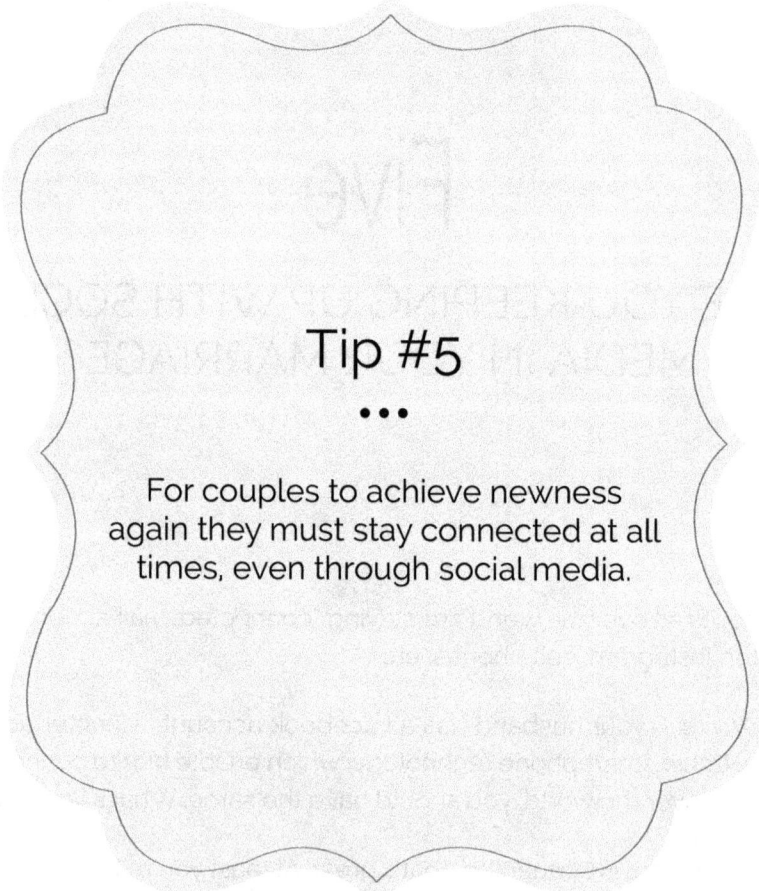

Tip #5

•••

For couples to achieve newness again they must stay connected at all times, even through social media.

Couples, YOU CAN ACHIEVE NEWNESS AGAIN!

Six

HOW HAPPY ARE YOU IN YOUR MARRIAGE?

Research shows that on a scale of one to ten, most people rate their marital happiness at a three. Yet, the United States of America's divorce rate hovers around fifty percent.

What can be done to bring your happiness quotient to at least an eight, and possibly even a ten? I have a few suggestions:

- Both spouses must forget past hurts, whatever they were, if they plan to stay married.
- Husbands should remember how they felt when they first saw their wives, and why they asked them to marry in the first place.
- Wives should remember how they felt when they were first asked to be married by their husbands.
- Both spouses must compliment each other on a regular basis. It won't kill a husband to tell his wife her new hair color is pretty. It won't kill a wife to tell her husband his new jeans fit nicely. The point is this: Stop taking each other for granted.

Six: How Happy Are You In Your Marriage?

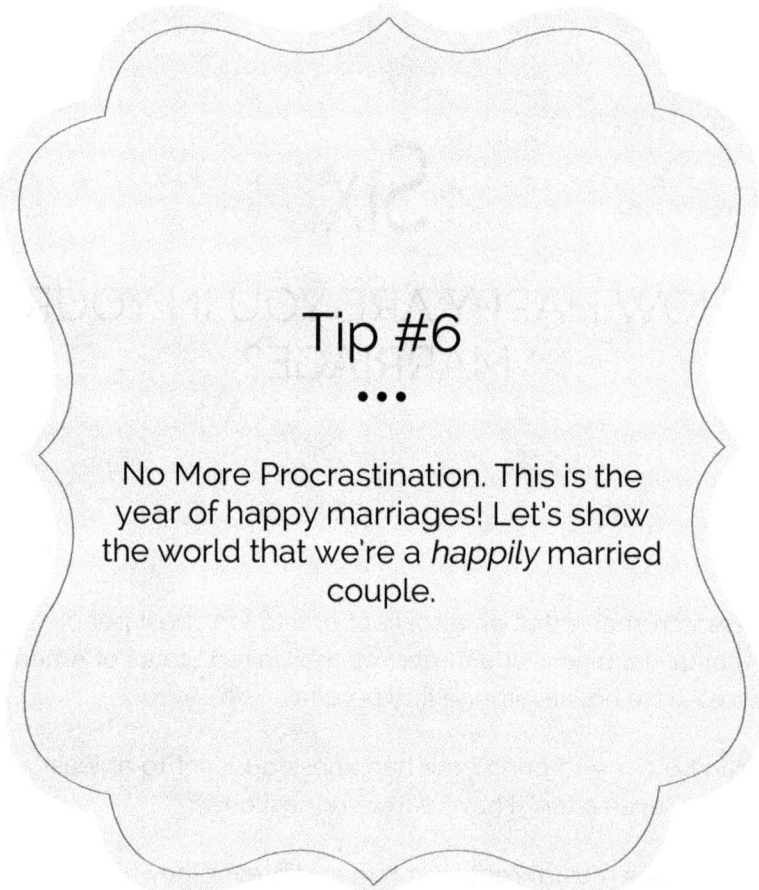

Tip #6

•••

No More Procrastination. This is the year of happy marriages! Let's show the world that we're a *happily* married couple.

Couples, YOU CAN ACHIEVE NEWNESS AGAIN!

Seven

IS JEALOUSY HOLDING YOUR MARRIAGE BACK?

The word jealousy has many meanings and layers to it. We are going to focus on it in the context of marriage.

Jealousy is a human emotion that must stay in check in a marriage.

According to Betty W. Phillips, Ph.D., Psychology, jealousy originates in a feeling (human emotion) that one has an advantage over the other, and its effect is insecurity. It also causes bondage; since your jealousy won't let you be free! That is no way to LIVE.

The wife might want to go back to school or even get a job, but the husbands says no, without offering logical rationale. That could be the result of jealousy, and it may ignore the fact that if the wife goes back to school or gets a job, it benefits the husband because more money comes into the household.

Seven: Is Jealousy Holding Your Marriage Back?

The husband may want to go out, maybe once a month with his buddies or male friends, but the wife pouts about it for several days. That could be the result of jealousy, and it may ignore the fact that if the husband can go out with his buddies he's not likely to lie about his whereabouts at other times.

Seven: Is Jealousy Holding Your Marriage Back?

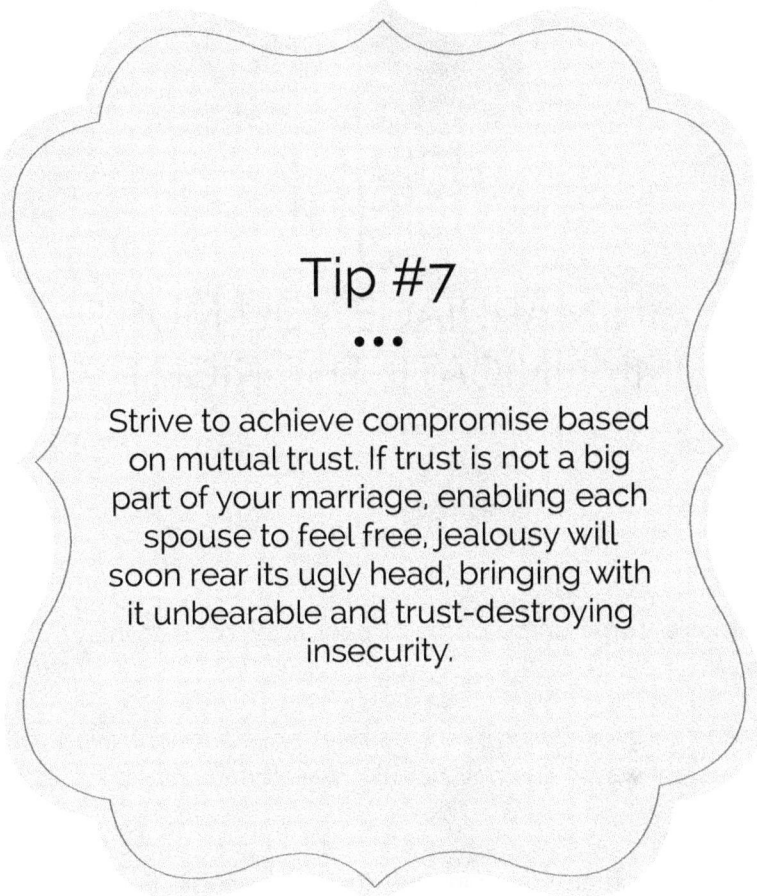

Tip #7

•••

Strive to achieve compromise based on mutual trust. If trust is not a big part of your marriage, enabling each spouse to feel free, jealousy will soon rear its ugly head, bringing with it unbearable and trust-destroying insecurity.

Couples, YOU CAN ACHIEVE NEWNESS AGAIN!

Eight

IN MARRIAGE YOU MUST COMMUNICATE THE RIGHT WAY

In marriage, communication must consist of heart-to-heart conversations.

So many couples spend precious days not communicating with each other the right way. If it is not the right way, then it can create havoc in a marriage.

Additionally, it creates a marriage-destroying habit. For example, husbands and wives not speaking to each other for a week is not only a bad habit, but is downright silly.

Three ways to communicate the right way:

1. Use a respectful tone of voice.
2. Listen without being dismissive of your spouse's expressed concerns.
3. Give your spouse a Hallmark, Mahogany, or other greeting card just because (don't wait for special occasions like Valentine's Day, Birthdays, etc.).

Eight: In Marriage You Must Communicate The Right Way

Tip #8
•••

If you both communicate the right way, your marriage will be on a journey that others will want to follow.

Couples, YOU CAN ACHIEVE NEWNESS AGAIN!

Nine

CAN TRAVELING WITH YOUR SPOUSE ENHANCE YOUR MARRIAGE?

A survey published in **USA Today** (2/7/13) conducted by the U.S. Travel Association found that couples who travel together have better relationships and better sex.

The question is when was the last time you and your spouse traveled out of town for a weekend alone?

Thanks to traveling together, couples reported that their relationships improved in the following ways:

1. Friendship & Closeness   (togetherness)   51% enjoyed it
2. Communication   (friendship)   43% enjoyed it
3. Patience & Flexibility   (relaxed) not tripping   41% enjoyed it

Sex ranked number seven, with twenty-eight percent of respondents saying sex improved, which indicates that although it wasn't the "main thing," traveling together resulted in an improved sex life for a significant number of couples.

Nine: Can Traveling With Your Spouse Enhance Your Marriage?

Tip #9

•••

For couples to achieve newness again, they should plan a weekend trip away, no matter the distance. I read a story where a couple was separated, so they decided to take a trip, while on that trip the husband says he remembered all of the reasons he got married. They re-connected on that trip and now they are celebrating eighteen years of marriage!

Couples, YOU CAN ACHIEVE NEWNESS AGAIN!

Ten

IS PARENTING WRECKING YOUR ROMANCE?

The answer is yes, if it is not done properly. Properly means both spouses must be on the same page.

The husband cannot say it is the wife's responsibility to take care of the children while he goes on with his regular routine.

Just like the notion of "falling in love," you will do whatever it takes for each other. It should be the same when children come into a relationship, you must do whatever it takes for each other. The challenge is to keep the relationship in tact as you raise your children and work. It requires a major adjustment, but it can be done:

1. By planning which parent will help with homework, music lessons, cook, clean up, wash clothes, take child to doctor, etc. One parent shouldn't have to do this if there are two in the home.

Ten: Is Parenting Wrecking Your Romance?

2. By scheduling time each week for each other, such as watching television together; having coffee together; and anything else you may enjoy doing together.
3. By going out on a monthly date. Schedule one starting this month. Dinner and a movie, maybe?

Ten: Is Parenting Wrecking Your Romance?

Tip #10

•••

It is your children's job to take up all of your time. It is your job to figure out creative ways to have a little fun without the children!

Couples, YOU CAN ACHIEVE NEWNESS AGAIN!

Eleven

WHICH DO HUSBANDS RANK FIRST: SEX OR A HOME-COOKED MEAL?

Both appetites are considered the most powerful of all human drives. Stanford University, and the Marriage Group, C.A.N.A. (Couples Achieving Newness Again) conducted separate surveys on feeding physical and sexual hunger.

According to the study by Stanford, these two appetites were on the same footing. Husbands want both equally.

According to the survey by the husbands of C.A.N.A., sex ranks first.

However, it is up to both spouses to decide together what they want:

- If one spouse wants sex, and the other wants a home-cooked meal a compromise must be reached. You will either dim the lights in the bedroom, or light up the stove in the kitchen for home-cooked breakfast, lunch, or dinner (but not all three).

Eleven: Which Do Husbands Rank First: Sex Or A Home-Cooked Meal?

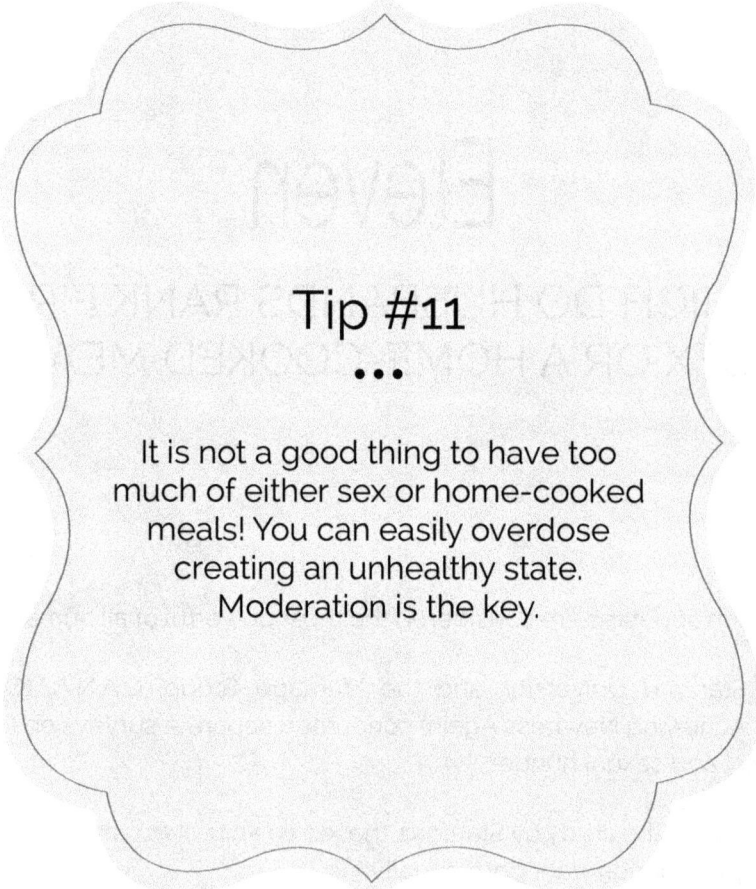

Tip #11
...
It is not a good thing to have too much of either sex or home-cooked meals! You can easily overdose creating an unhealthy state. Moderation is the key.

Couples, YOU CAN ACHIEVE NEWNESS AGAIN!

Twelve

HOW DO YOU KEEP PEACE IN YOUR MARRIAGE?

According to an article published, entitled "Know your Anger" by Creative Process Counseling Services, you keep peace in your marriage by controlling your level of anger.

Anger can build up from level 1 to level 10, causing serious damage to your marriage.

The anger levels are in this order:

1. First, you feel uneasy
2. Then you feel uncomfortable
3. Then you just shut down (become withdrawn)
4. You feel irritated
5. You feel agitated
6. You feel annoyed
7. You get upset

Twelve: How Do You Keep Peace In Your Marriage?

8. Then you are mad
9. You are angry
10. Then you are furious or full of rage

If you get to level seven, you have already gone through the emotions of levels 1-6, which is not healthy. It means you have an issue where anger is too frequent, and lasts too long. It stops you and your marriage from growing.

Twelve: How Do You Keep Peace In Your Marriage?

Tip #12
•••

You keep peace in your marriage by stopping at the "uneasy" stage, and immediately communicating to your spouse what it is that is making you uneasy.

Always allow peace to propel your marriage forward into the future.

Couples, YOU CAN ACHIEVE NEWNESS AGAIN!

Thirteen

ARE YOU FLIRTING OUTSIDE OF YOUR MARRIAGE?

Elizabeth Bernstein, in a December 2012 article in The Wall Street Journal, made note to something said by one of her interview subjects – noted as Ms. Russell, "But flirting is a fast, inexpensive way to have a better day."

I am sure we all know when we are flirting, but we probably also do not think deeply enough about its meaning.

Flirting is ambiguous behavior with sexual or romantic overtones.

Flirting is a good thing if you are single and flirting with a single person.

It is also a good thing if you are married and flirting with your spouse, but so often it is twisted.

That same Wall Street Journal article stated people flirt for six fundamental reasons:

1. Looking for a mate
2. They enjoy it
3. It is fun (of course it is!)
4. They want to explore a romantic relationship
5. They want to boost their self-esteem
6. They flirt to get what they want

Thirteen: Are You Flirting Outside Of Your Marriage?

Tip #13

...

Flirting outside of your marriage can cause serious problems, but flirting inside your marriage can keep it healthy.

Couples, YOU CAN ACHIEVE NEWNESS AGAIN!

Fourteen

SHOULD I FORGIVE OR FORGET?

We often hear people say, "I will forgive, but I won't forget." This statement is typically heard in marriage when the husband or the wife has done something contrary to the wedding vows.

What does that statement mean? It means I will no longer resent you for what you did to me, but I will always remember what you did. This way of thinking is not healthy - if you plan to stay in your marriage.

You must *forgive* and *forget*. They go together. It may be hard to do, but it is necessary. If you forget without forgiving, you will not experience the joy of marriage. Further, the incident, which led to the unforgiveness, will always be a part of your marital relationship.

Fourteen: Should I Forgive Or Forget?

Tip #14

•••

Don't let it be too late to say,
"I forgive, and I forget."

Couples, YOU CAN ACHIEVE NEWNESS AGAIN!

Fifteen

IN MARRIAGE, CAN WHAT YOU WEAR TO BED AFFECT YOUR RELATIONSHIP?

The answer is Yes. It can affect your relationship in a positive or negative way.

I have been hearing from some husbands who say they need their wives to do better when it comes to what they wear to bed.

When they first got married, there were so many beautiful negligees - Pink, blue, black, red, and orange ones. After a while, those beautiful and colorful negligees started disappearing. The husbands say they started seeing more pajama pants, gym pants, and other unattractive clothing for bed.

Some husbands admitted that they even think of their mothers when their wives wear the unattractive clothing at bedtime.

They say that if the wife could wear a negligee to bed just once a week, life would be perfect.

Husbands, I have a question for you: Is there a reason the wife is not wearing a negligee as often as you would like?

Fifteen: In Marriage, Can What You Wear To Bed Affect Your Relationship?

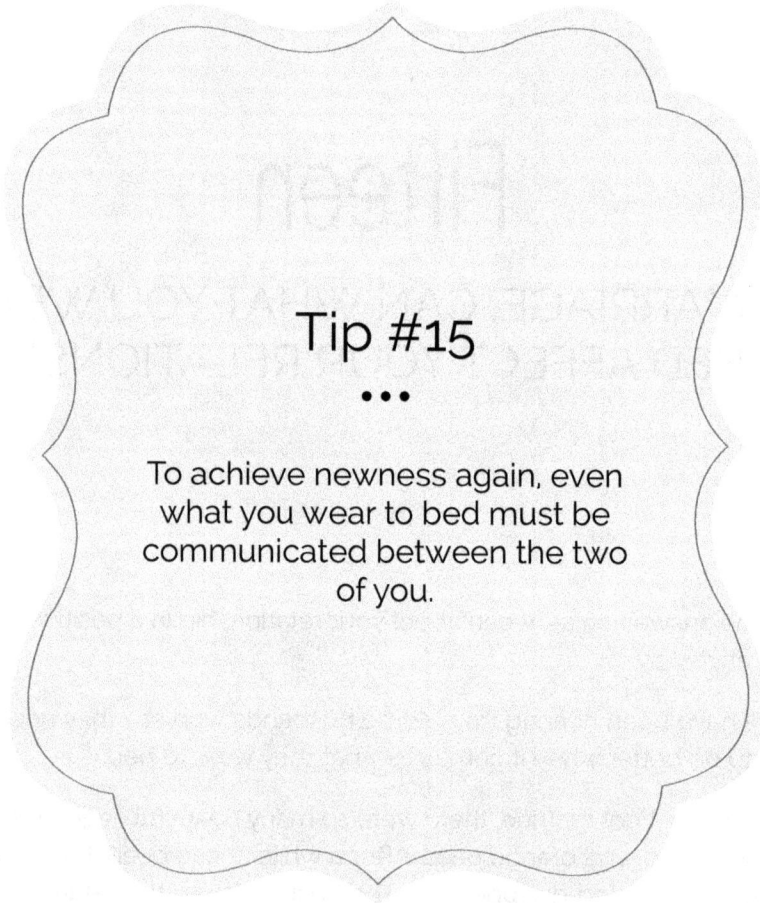

Tip #15

•••

To achieve newness again, even what you wear to bed must be communicated between the two of you.

Couples, YOU CAN ACHIEVE NEWNESS AGAIN!

Sixteen
DO YOU TRUST YOUR SPOUSE?

The traditional wedding vows use words such as *love, comfort, and honor, keep in sickness, and in health, forsaking all others, keep yourself only to him/her, for better or for worse, richer, or poorer,* but I couldn't find the word trust.

There are three levels of trust, but the one that identifies with marriage, according to Randy Conley, in Leading with Trust is identity-based trust. This is the most intimate level of trust. If I trust you on this level, it means you know my hopes, dreams, goals, ambitions, fears, and doubts.

In marriage, when you trust someone you are saying, "You have earned the right to know everything about me. I am transparent, because you will not take advantage of me."

However, when either spouse in the marriage misuses this level of trust, it will almost take a miracle to get this trust back.

Sixteen: Do You Trust Your Spouse?

Another kind of trust is deterrence-based trust. This one is the most fundamental base level of trust in all relationships. There are rules in place that prevent one person from taking advantage of, or harming another person.

The third kind of trust is knowledge-based trust. This level of trust means that I've had enough experience with you and knowledge of your behavior that I have a good idea of how you will react and behave in relationship with me.

Sixteen: Do You Trust Your Spouse?

Tip #16

•••

If you want to achieve newness again, you must believe in miracles!

Couples, YOU CAN ACHIEVE NEWNESS AGAIN!

Seventeen

DOES THE SILENT TREATMENT HELP OR HURT YOUR MARRIAGE?

Ignoring your spouse or giving your spouse the cold shoulder for days at a time can hurt your marriage in a big way.

The silent treatment shows up in three ways: Abuse, lack of communication, and wasted time.

Somebody is the perpetrator and somebody is the victim.

Marriage Expert, Sheri Stritof says, "Ignoring your spouse is a cop-out with both spouses in different ways."

Both husbands and wives are emotional and sensitive, but the wife is more emotional so she may just stop talking all together concerning an issue.

The husband is more sensitive and does not want to feel inadequate to his spouse on an issue so he would rather be quiet than say the wrong thing.

Seventeen: Does The Silent Treatment Help Or Hurt Your Marriage?

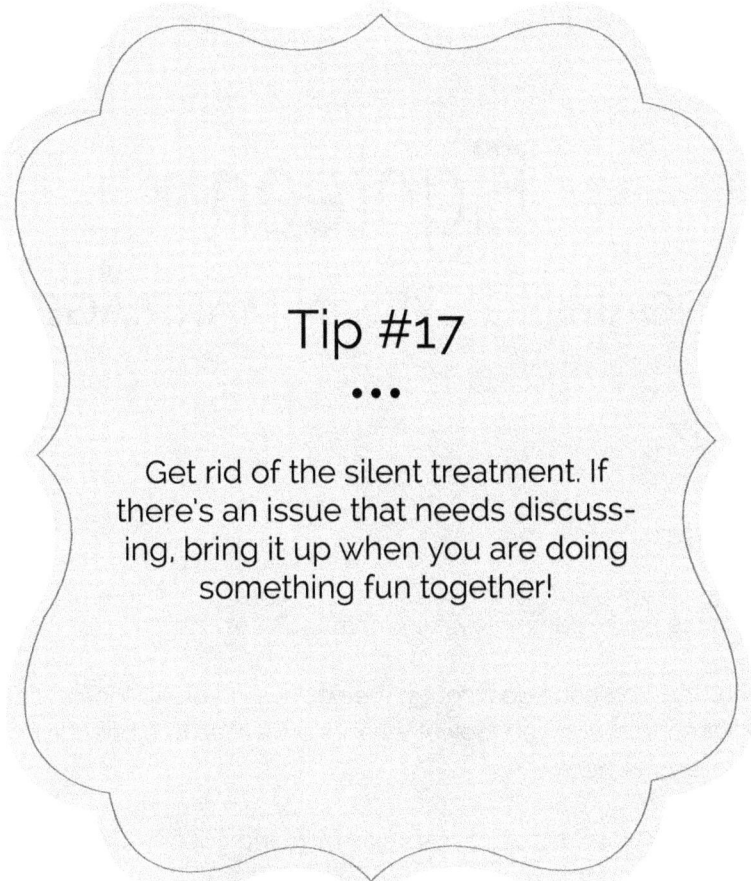

Tip #17

Get rid of the silent treatment. If there's an issue that needs discussing, bring it up when you are doing something fun together!

Couples, YOU CAN ACHIEVE NEWNESS AGAIN!

Eighteen
ROAMING EYES IN MARRIAGE

Is it okay to have roaming eyes in marriage? Yes!

It is natural. You can't go through life not being able to look at someone else. Of course, you can look at a handsome man or a beautiful woman. They are everywhere.

However, don't disrespect your spouse by going out of your way to get the attention of another.

Complimenting someone other than your spouse works the same way. The problem is that some husbands compliment other women, more than they compliment their wives. This is not a good thing. The husband that does this is out of line.

Eighteen: Roaming Eyes In Marriage

Tip #18
...

To achieve newness again, keep your eyes on your spouse (most of the time), when you are in his or her presence.

Couples, YOU CAN ACHIEVE NEWNESS AGAIN!

Nineteen

TAKING EXTREME MEASURES TO SAVE YOUR MARRIAGE

The book, *Living Happily Ever After/Separately*, by Lise Stoessel, reports that some couples are taking extreme measures to keep their marriages alive.

The book gives the example of one spouse leaving the house they lived in together for years and buying his or her own house to live separately from their spouse. Yet they see each other on a regular basis.

Alternatively, each spouse has his or her own bedroom in the same house. They don't sleep in the same bed on a regular basis. The stated reason is that they don't want to be bothered with snoring, the remote control, the computer, and any other interruptions.

Third, eating dark chocolate on a regular basis - and not just once a year - on Valentine's Day does wonders. Eating chocolates affects your moods, energy, sexual functions, and your heart in remarkable ways. It increases blood flow, which makes you come alive. In addition, it is not as fattening as other chocolates.

Nineteen: Taking Extreme Measures To Save Your Marriage

Tip #19

•••

Each spouse must talk to each other before enforcing any measures.

Couples, YOU CAN ACHIEVE NEWNESS AGAIN!

Twenty

DO PETS HELP OR HURT YOUR MARRIAGE?

Let me first say, I realize pet owners love their pets very much, and many treat them as family members. We had Romeo, Jazzy, and Kodie in the Whalum Family!

With that said, pets can help and hurt a marriage. A study performed by the University of Buffalo claims that having a pet in your home can actually help in various regards. Couples who own a dog or a cat tend to have a closer relationship with each other. Another study showed that patting your pet could even lower blood pressure.

Having a pet can also hurt your marriage. A pet can create many problems in the marriage.

Many spouses feel closer to the family pet than to their spouse. These spouses speak better to their pets than to the one to whom they are mar-

Twenty: Do Pets Help Or Hurt Your Marriage?

ried. They make sure the pet has his/her food. The spouse makes sure the pet is comfortable and often the pet is touched and patted.

One spouse often feels jealous of the pet because he or she believes the pet is receiving all of the attention. So, what should that spouse do that feels that way?

Tell the spouse how you feel. You may say that is silly, but it is not. It is a real problem, which requires resolution. In order to achieve newness again, nothing and no one should be closer to you than the one with whom you share a life commitment.

Twenty: Do Pets Help Or Hurt Your Marriage?

Tip #20
•••

The pet just may have to leave the home. Yes, marriage is that important.

Couples, YOU CAN ACHIEVE NEWNESS AGAIN!

Twenty-one
WHY THE NEED TO HYPHENATE YOUR NAME? IS THIS THE NEW NORM?

History records that for many years, the wife would gladly take her husband's last name when they got married. Then things started changing in society. Wives began to leave behind the title of homemaker, and became producers of television shows, businesswomen, doctors, lawyers, politicians; you name it.

Wives gave three reasons why they wanted to hyphenate their name:

1. Submission was hard for her. "You are not the boss of me."
2. She wanted to maintain her own identity and stay connected to what she had accomplished.
3. A contingency plan in case of divorce.

Research mentioned in an article on the website, www.marriagenamechange.com, shows that a large portion of today's society does not agree with this position, still a large portion of wives who maintain their

Twenty-one: Why The Need To Hyphenate Your Name? Is This The New Norm?

last name and add the husbands are considered to be strong and do not care what others think.

Will this position of those wives who hyphenate their name make for happy marriages? Possibly, but, only if both partners agree. However, the article says, "It is possible that your future husband will find this choice offensive." Therefore, you should consider this and make a relationship-healthy decision.

Twenty-one: Why The Need To Hyphenate Your Name? Is This The New Norm?

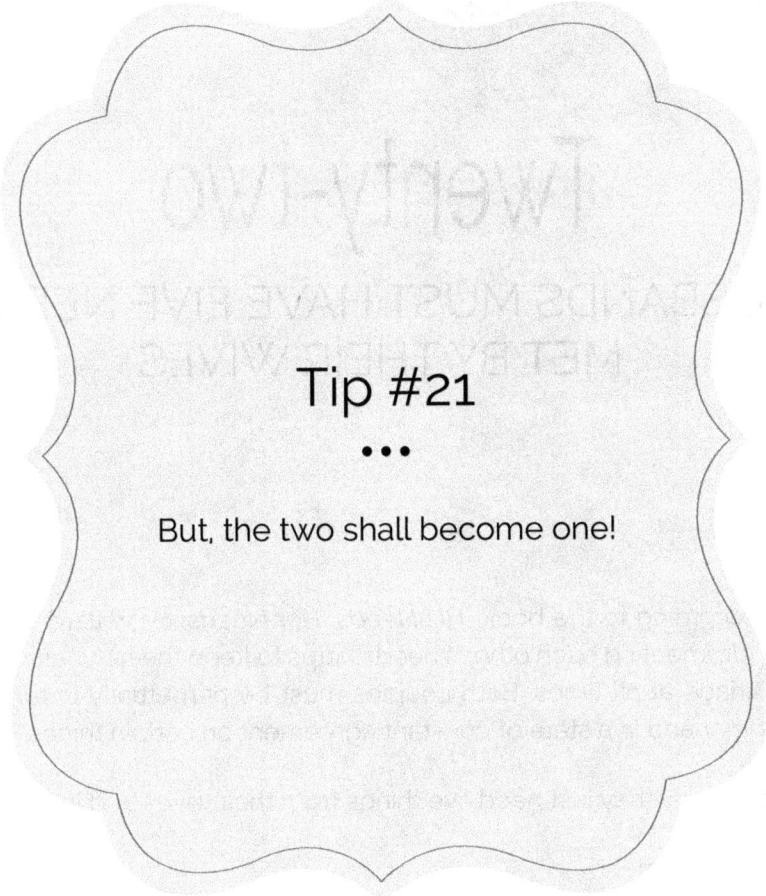

Tip #21

...

But, the two shall become one!

Couples, YOU CAN ACHIEVE NEWNESS AGAIN!

Twenty-two

HUSBANDS MUST HAVE FIVE NEEDS MET BY THEIR WIVES

According to the book, *His Needs, Her Needs*, by Willard F. Harley Jr., meeting each other's needs helps to keep the newness in marriage at all times. Both couples must be perpetually in tune with each other and in a state of constant agreement on certain things.

Husbands say they just need five things from their wives and in this order:

1. Sexual fulfillment;
2. Recreational companionship;
3. Attractiveness;
4. Home support/clean house, cooking, etc.;
5. Admiration.

Twenty-two: Husbands Must Have Five Needs Met By Their Wives

Wives say they need the following five things from their husbands:

1. Affection;
2. Conversation;
3. Honesty;
4. Financial Support;
5. Family Commitment.

Notice that the list is not the same for husbands and wives, which means there are at least ten needs that need consideration in your efforts to keep your marriage strong. If you don't agree with these lists, create your own, because you're going to need them!

Twenty-two: Husbands Must Have Five Needs Met By Their Wives

Tip #22

•••

Three questions:

Who is keeping up with this list?

Have you communicated it with each other?

Are you willing to put in the work for your marriage?

Couples, YOU CAN ACHIEVE NEWNESS AGAIN!

Twenty-three

DO YOU HAVE A STRATEGY TO STAY MARRIED?

Memphian R. Brad Martin, Interim President of the University of Memphis and retired Chairman and CEO of Saks, Incorporated, along with Reverend Shane Stanford, Senior Pastor of Christ United Methodist Church, co-published a book entitled, **Five Stones: Conquering Your Giants.**

It is a dynamic book, but what really caught my attention was when Brad stated, he had a strategy for everything but his marriage. He did not pay attention to the warning signs. His first marriage ended after twenty-four years.

Martin says he was making plans for his business, kids, homes and community service, but not for his marriage. He has remarried, and now understands that his marriage comes first.

Twenty-three: Do You Have A Strategy To Stay Married?

A strategic plan lays out the method to be used in order to achieve a particular goal:

1. We must contemplate our plans. Now that you are married, now what?
2. Will you work 8 hours, then come home and help with cooking?
3. Develop a plan based on your own marriage, dealing with children, jobs, school, etc.;
4. Will you agree together on how you will raise your child(ren)?
5. Update your plan often - together.
6. Will you revisit your plan annually to stay on track?

Twenty-three: Do You Have A Strategy To Stay Married?

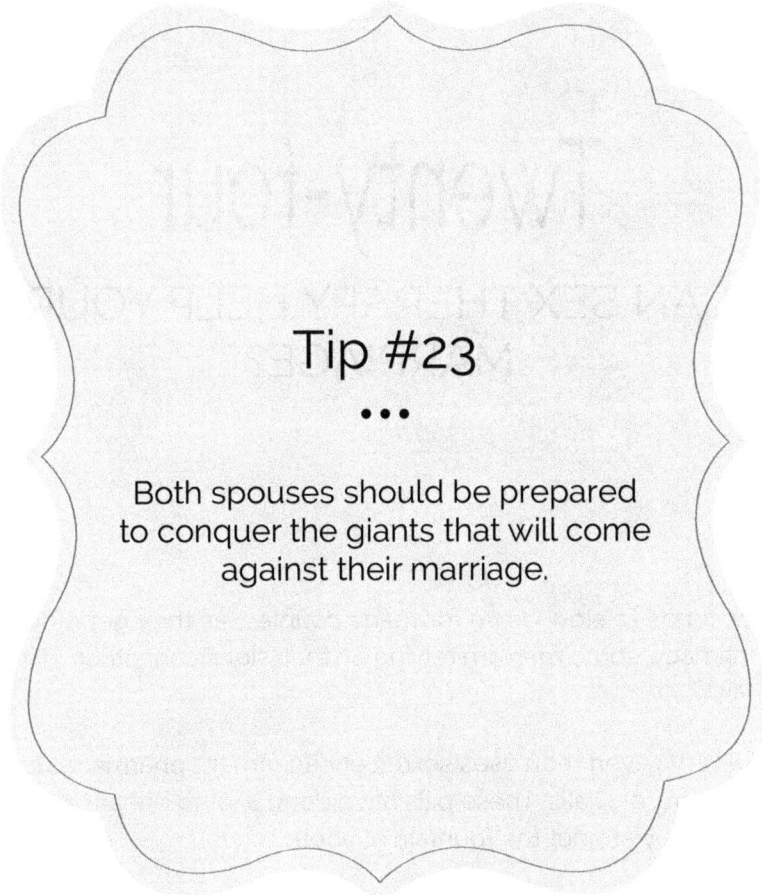

Tip #23
•••

Both spouses should be prepared to conquer the giants that will come against their marriage.

Couples, YOU CAN ACHIEVE NEWNESS AGAIN!

Twenty-four

CAN SEX THERAPY HELP YOUR MARRIAGE?

Sex tends to slow down for many couples, as they get older, so for intimacy, some men are relying on their significant other: The Purple Pill.

One of every seven men uses sexual enhancement pharmaceuticals like Viagra, Levitra, or Cialis. These pills have done a lot to enhance sexual capacity, but they are not the fountain of youth.

If a husband has to take any of these pills, then the wife must know about it because not only are they expensive, they do have some serious potential side effects.

Dr. Michael Perelman, Co-Director of the Human Sexuality program at New York Presbyterian Hospital, created the Sexual Tipping Point Model.

He explains that the average man spends two to three years in denial about his dysfunction because often sex was everything to him in his younger days. There should be no shame because it's normal: age, diabetes, and high blood pressure are often major factors of the dysfunction.

Dr. Perelman states that wives should be more sensitive to their husbands because it is the same as wives going through menopause. Wives should not embarrass their husbands over this issue.

Twenty-four: Can Sex Therapy Help Your Marriage?

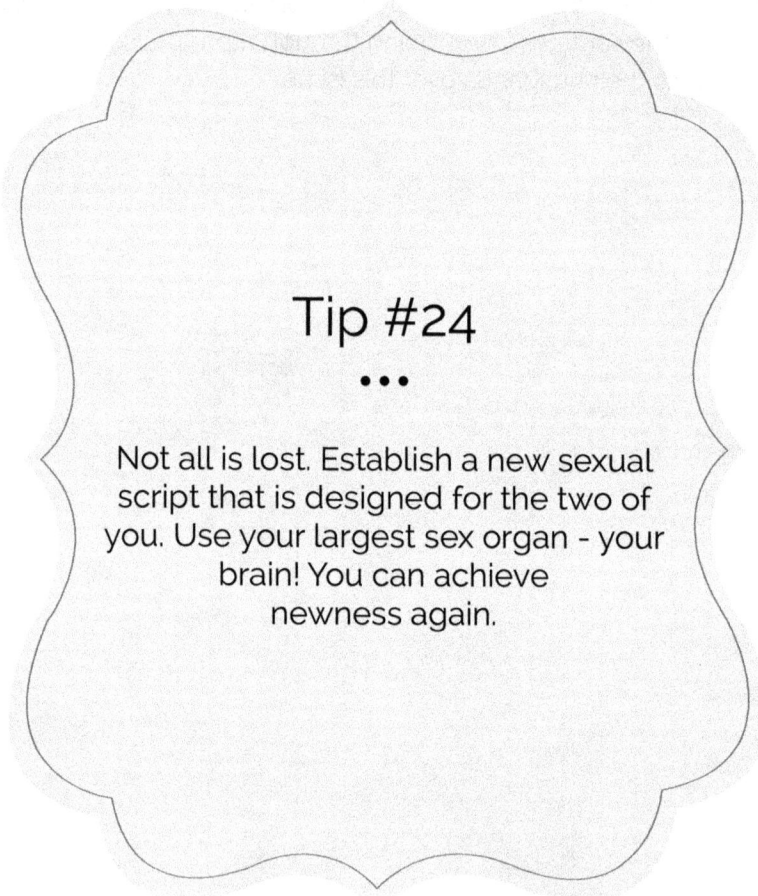

Tip #24
•••

Not all is lost. Establish a new sexual script that is designed for the two of you. Use your largest sex organ - your brain! You can achieve newness again.

Couples, YOU CAN ACHIEVE NEWNESS AGAIN!

Twenty-five
IS KISSING STILL IMPORTANT IN MARRIAGE?

Most traditional weddings conclude with the phrase, "You may kiss the bride."

Ironically, research shows (Huffington Post survey) that after the bride becomes the wife, kissing ceases to be high on the husband's list of things to do anymore. Married Couples kiss less than once a week.

During courtship, men loved to kiss their girlfriends, and their girlfriends looked forward to it, but after marriage, the husband does not initiate it as he once did. He can take it or leave it according to a study done by New York University.

However, husbands may want to reconsider because kissing helps the brain.

When you kiss, your whole body feels good and satisfied.

Research also shows that couples who kissed for thirty minutes at a time, experienced healing of all kinds of problems.

Twenty-five: Is Kissing Still Important In Marriage?

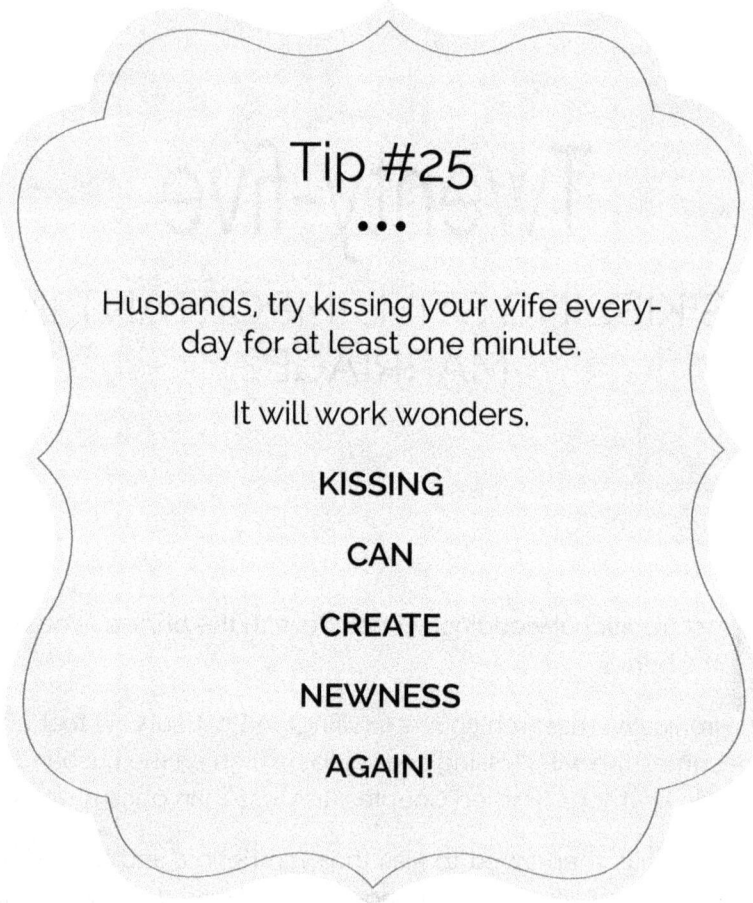

Tip #25

...

Husbands, try kissing your wife everyday for at least one minute.

It will work wonders.

KISSING

CAN

CREATE

NEWNESS

AGAIN!

Couples, YOU CAN ACHIEVE NEWNESS AGAIN!

Twenty-six

DO YOU KNOW YOUR SPOUSE'S LOVE LANGUAGES?

Don't assume your spouse knows what you want. Tell or show your spouse what you desire, crave, need - want.

Author Gary Chapman, wrote in his book, *The Five Love Languages*, that there are at least five languages you should be using with your spouse. Are you using those listed below?

- Love Language #1 - Words of Affirmation
- Love Language #2 - Quality Time
- Love Language #3 - Receiving Gifts
- Love Language #4 - Acts of Service
- Love Language #5 - Physical Touch

1. Words of Affirmation: Speak loving words to your spouse, at least every now and then.
2. Quality Time: Give undivided attention to each other.

Twenty-six: Do You Know Your Spouse's Love Languages?

3. Receiving Gifts: Gift-giving is a part of the love-marriage process. It is more than just holidays and birthdays.
4. Acts of Service: Doing things your spouse would love for you to do, like painting a bedroom.
5. Physical Touch: Communicate marital love through touch. Without it your spouse feels unloved.

Tip #26

•••

Discover your spouse's primary love language(s) in order to achieve newness again!

Couples, YOU CAN ACHIEVE NEWNESS AGAIN!

Twenty-seven

WHY DID ELIZABETH TAYLOR MARRY EIGHT TIMES?

Elizabeth Taylor, considered one of the most beautiful women in the world, was famous for that beauty and her love life. She married eight times, one husband she actually married twice.

Their names:

1. Mr. Hilton
2. Mr. Wilding
3. Mr. Todd
4. Mr. Fisher
5. Mr. Burton (twice)
7. Mr. Warner
8. Mr. Fortensky

Why did Liz marry so many times?

Twenty-seven: Why Did Elizabeth Taylor Marry Eight Times?

She probably married so many times because she loved the "feeling" of "falling in love." Falling in love is not the same kind of love that exists in marriage.

When you "fall in love," it's a strong sense of attraction towards one another. You let go of all preconceived notions.

When you have been married for some time, that strong sense of attraction changes into many *dis*tractions, and that feeling of falling in love is buried.

Twenty-seven: Why Did Elizabeth Taylor Marry Eight Times?

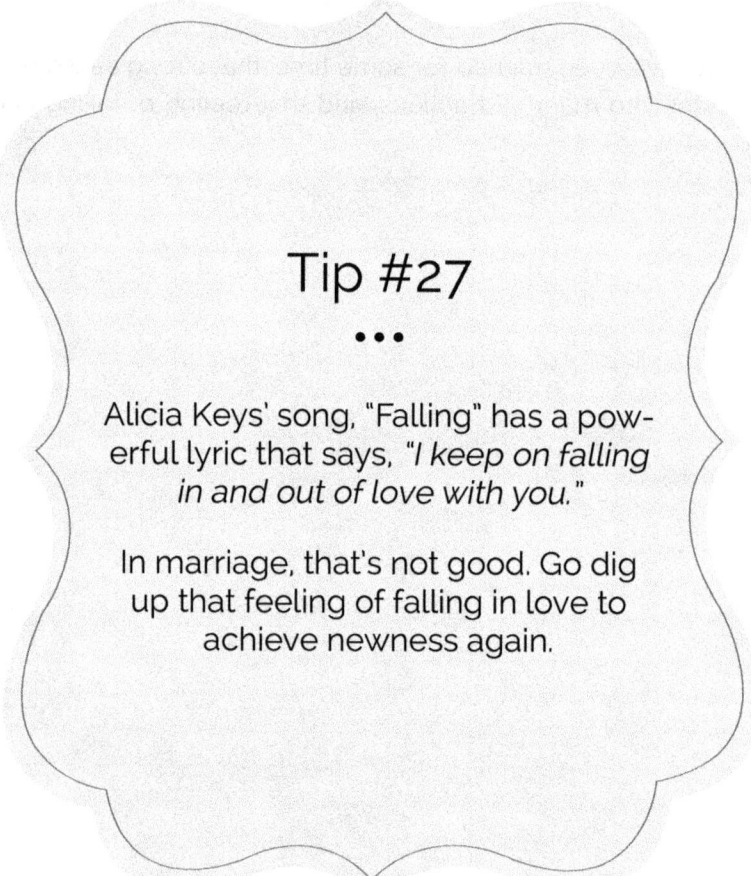

Tip #27

•••

Alicia Keys' song, "Falling" has a powerful lyric that says, *"I keep on falling in and out of love with you."*

In marriage, that's not good. Go dig up that feeling of falling in love to achieve newness again.

Couples, YOU CAN ACHIEVE NEWNESS AGAIN!

Twenty-eight
IS IT MY MONEY, OR OUR MONEY?

In marriage, you become one, and what is his is mine and what is mine is his, including *our* money.

There may be five checkbooks between the two of you, but all the accounts belong to both of you.

You may have an account for the main expenses, and then for personal expenses, however, both spouses should be able to follow the money and know where it is going at all times.

It is very important to know who is best at handling the money in your marriage and also very important to meet at least once a month with your spouse to discuss money matters.

First comes love, then marriage, then money. Forty-five percent of married couples end up divorcing over money matters because they didn't have a serious discussion about money before they got married.

Twenty-eight: Is It My Money, Or Our Money?

Tip #28

•••

On your joint account, the husband's name should appear first on all checks.

Also:
Would you marry someone with a bad
FICO Score (Fair Isaac Corporation)?
Yes! If you love that person, you can help him/her raise that score.
Here's a helpful guide to FICO scores:
580 is bad
710 is average
740 is good
800 is excellent

This score shows how tall you are standing. A credit rating is an assessment of a person's creditworthiness, and gives an indication of how likely he/she is to pay their debts.

Couples, YOU CAN ACHIEVE NEWNESS AGAIN!

Twenty-nine

THE AGE FACTOR IN MARRIAGE: DOES IT MATTER?

R&B artist Jaheim had a hit song called "Age Ain't A Factor." The legal age to get married is eighteen in most states. Statistics from the Pew Research Center show that first-time marriages from the period of 1960-2011 occurred between couples of about 20 and 25 years old respectively, a five-year difference between the husband and the wife with the husband, being older. "Today, just 20% of adults ages 18 to 29 are married, compared with 59% in 1960," the research shows.

However, if there is a divorce from the first marriage, some have given marriage another try - marrying two, three or four more times.

Often, a wife will have a husband of maybe five to ten years younger than she is, while a husband will have a wife maybe twenty-five years younger than he is.

There's nothing wrong with so-called "May/December" marriages, but just know it takes more work to make the marriage work when there is such a big age gap. Many reasons are given for this age gap, but the main thing is to have someone to love and share your life.

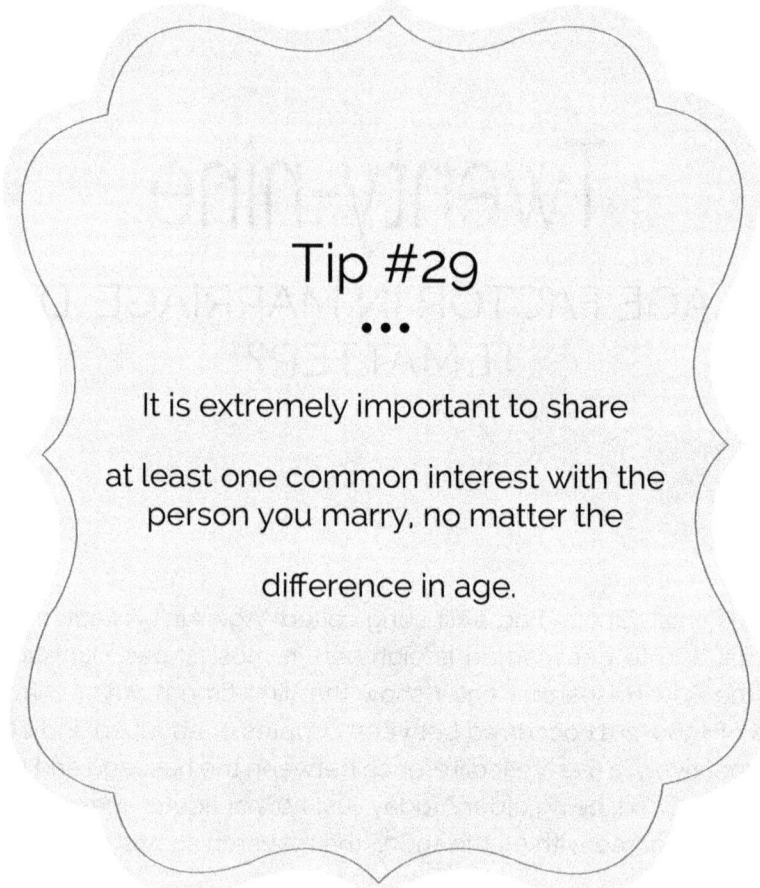

Tip #29

...

It is extremely important to share

at least one common interest with the person you marry, no matter the

difference in age.

Couples, YOU CAN ACHIEVE NEWNESS AGAIN!

Thirty

IS YOUR MARRIAGE STUCK IN "THE CRAZY CYCLE?"

In order to achieve newness again, Dr. Emerson Eggerichs suggests in his book, **Love and Respect** that both spouses need to get off the crazy cycle. The crazy cycle describes the negative reactions that arise when conflicts come into the marriage.

He writes, "If the wife is on the crazy cycle, she often feels she is not being loved, and so she reacts or attacks her husband with words or anything else that she thinks will hurt him.

If the husband is on the crazy cycle, then he often feels disrespected by his wife, so he reacts or attacks his wife with words or anything else that he thinks will hurt her."

If both spouses are on the crazy cycle at the same time, that is not good. So, one of you need to get off and then help the other one get off.

Thirty: Is Your Marriage Stuck In "The Crazy Cycle?"

Tip #30

•••

Get off the crazy cycle right now! Have eyes to see and ears to hear. In other words, pay attention to each other.

Couples, YOU CAN ACHIEVE NEWNESS AGAIN!

Thirty-one

IS SEPARATION GOOD OR BAD FOR YOUR MARRIAGE?

A ny time you have to leave the home because you are not getting along, is not a good thing.

My research shows that at least three things could happen when a couple separates. According to Matthew B. Tully, in a special article for Military Times:

1. A spouse could commit and be convicted of adultery. When you separate, you are actually living the single life, even though you are legally married. When you forget you are married, things happen.

According to The People's Law Library of Maryland,
2. A spouse could move forward with divorce proceedings based on a 12-month separation. If a spouse moves out it could possibly hinder attempts at reconciliation.

As seen in the weekly C.A.N.A. (Couples Achieving Newness Again) class,
3. Both spouses could commit to renewing their relationship. A separation could make one spouse realize that they really do love their spouse, and cause them to commit to reconciliation.

Thirty-one: Is Separation Good Or Bad For Your Marriage?

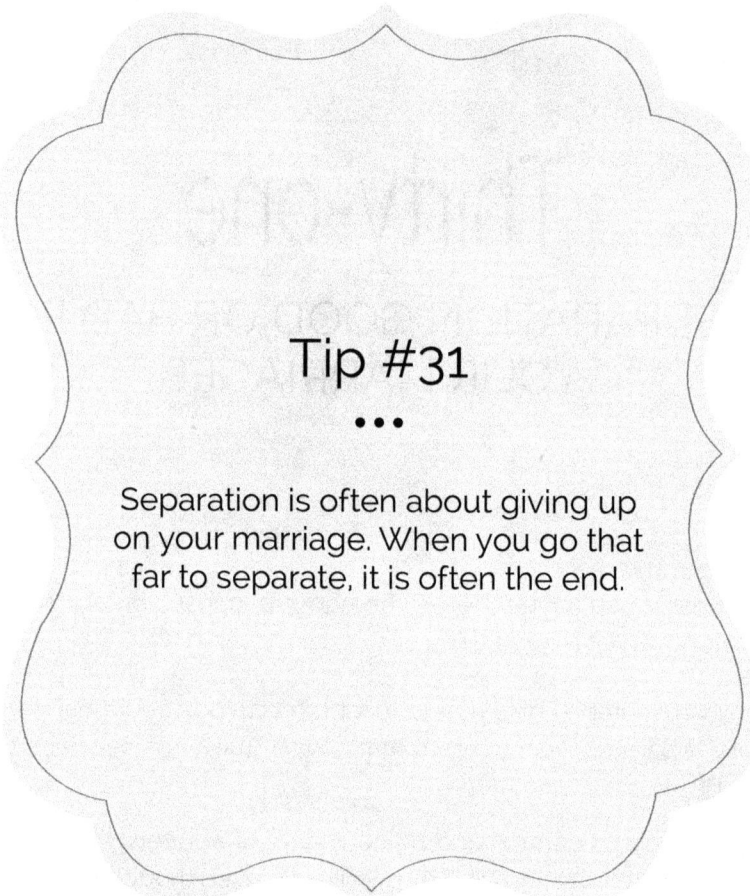

Tip #31

•••

Separation is often about giving up on your marriage. When you go that far to separate, it is often the end.

Couples, YOU CAN ACHIEVE NEWNESS AGAIN!

Thirty-two

DO YOU AND YOUR SPOUSE SHARE THE SAME RELIGION?
(RELIGION IS DEFINED AS BELIEF IN A DEITY OR A DIVINE PERSON)

Many couples do, and many couples do not. The reason is because many see religion as a personal thing and that they do not have to answer to anyone about that part of their lives. However, when you become married, as is often stated, you become one. Therefore, it is very important that you decide how you will handle this part of your lives.

There are several dynamics:

1. One spouse may be a Christian and one may be a Jew
2. One may be a Christian and one may be a Muslim
3. One may be a Christian and one may be a Catholic
4. One may be a Christian and one may not have a religion
5. Or, Both spouses may not have a religion at all.

My rule of thumb is, "Whatever Works!"

Thirty-two: Do You And Your Spouse Share The Same Religion?

Religion is just like voting rights. It is your individual right to believe what you want to believe. However, both spouses should be accepting of the other's choice. If you don't accept the religion of your spouse, you must know it will create a negative impact on your marriage.

Tip #32
...
Your religious beliefs should be making you a better spouse.

Couples, YOU CAN ACHIEVE NEWNESS AGAIN!

Thirty-three

WHEN WAS THE LAST TIME YOUR HUSBAND OPENED THE CAR DOOR FOR YOU?

When this act of kindness is shown all of the time, your marriage can get better.

Some may say that is so old-fashioned, but it is proper!

Opening the door for your wife does three things:

1. It makes a statement that you *value* her.
2. It means you *honor* her.
3. It means that you *cover/protect* her.

The main point is that many young boys didn't learn this during their childhood, so as they became men, they didn't know it was an indication of chivalry, which women look for in mates.

Unfortunately, many women are so independent, that they open the door for themselves even when a man is around. *Really!*

Thirty-three: When Was The Last Time Your Husband Opened The Car Door For You?

Tip #33

...

This free service does wonders for a relationship.

Couples, YOU CAN ACHIEVE NEWNESS AGAIN!

Thirty-four
DO YOU NEED A MARRIAGE COUNSELOR?

If you experience any of the following seven things, you probably do. Research shows that just one of these signs can destroy your marriage:

1. Poor communication;
2. Sex life has drastically changed;
3. Holding on to the past;
4. Bringing up the same issue repeatedly;
5. Financial disagreements;
6. Parenting styles;
7. If you still love your spouse, but something is missing.

What do you do before it is too late?

1. Meet with a licensed marriage counselor
2. Meet with a Pastor or other spiritual leader
3. Have a "C.A.N.A." meeting where you meet in a group with other married couples and talk about the issue(s). (You should attend together)

Thirty-four: Do You Need A Marriage Counselor?

Tip #34

...

Decide together if the marriage is worth saving. Don't just walk away.

Couples, YOU CAN ACHIEVE NEWNESS AGAIN!

Thirty-five

ARE YOU INTO PDA'S (PUBLIC DISPLAYS OF AFFECTION) FOR OR FROM YOUR SPOUSE?

1. Wearing clothing such as t-shirts that say "I Love My Husband," or "I Love My Wife." (I wear my "I Love My Husband" t-shirt often.)
2. Hugging in public;
3. Touching in public;
4. Tattoos (like the ones Jay-Z and Beyoncé have!); They both wear the IV symbol on their wedding finger, which reminds them of Jay-Z's December 4th birthday; Beyonce's September 4th birthday and their April 4th wedding anniversary.
5. Wearing matching outfits or colors when you go out in public (I know many married couples who do this);
6. Both spouses wearing their wedding rings in public.

Is it necessary to show the world how you feel about your spouse? Yes, but it should be G-rated for children. In addition, both spouses should agree. This issue should not be one-sided.

Thirty-five: Are You Into PDA's or From Your Spouse

In the *USA Today* the day after Valentine's Day, there was a story about a young couple in Pakistan who had to sneak around to express Valentine's Day greetings to each other, because PDAs are forbidden in their country. We have the freedom in America to express affection openly.

Thirty-five: Are You Into PDA's or From Your Spouse

Tip #35

•••

Try PDAs, especially during the love month of February.

Couples, YOU CAN ACHIEVE NEWNESS AGAIN!

Thirty-six

CAN A GLASS OF WINE ENHANCE YOUR MARRIAGE?

A study done by the health website *Sharecare* in 2013 says drinking alcohol is considered a social activity, and that Memphis women out-drink all women in the United States.

Two reasons are suggested for this pattern of drinking:

1. Women drink for health reasons.
2. Some wives started drinking to have a common interest with husbands, since the husbands could no longer frequent the bars as they once did when they were single.

As a way to allow the husband to continue to enjoy his beverage of choice, the wife would join her husband. This is time for both of them to "chill," if you will.

Thirty-six: Can A Glass Of Wine Enhance Your Marriage?

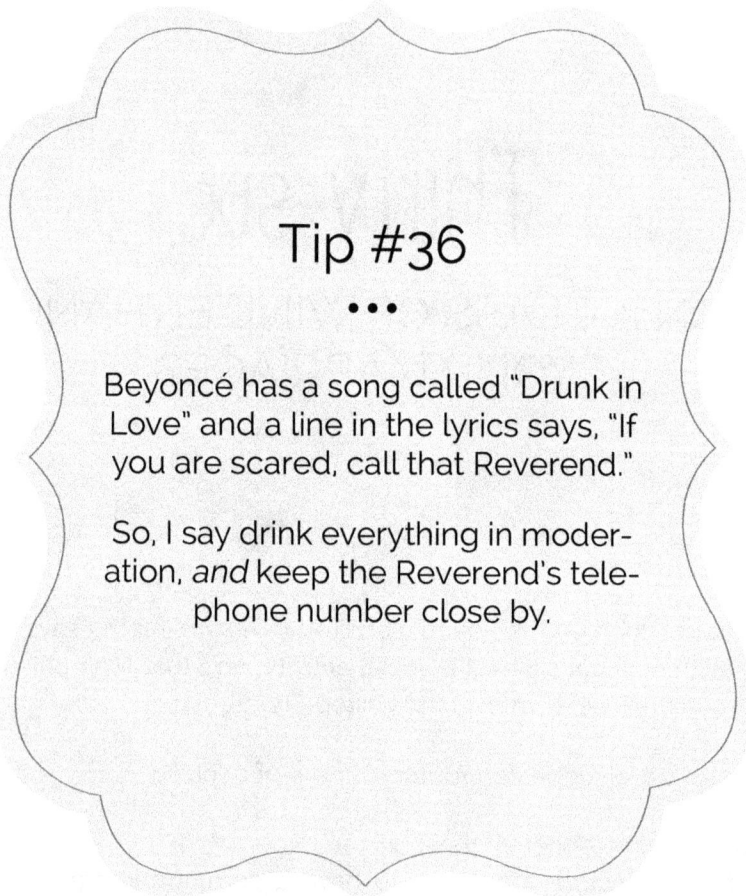

Tip #36

•••

Beyoncé has a song called "Drunk in Love" and a line in the lyrics says, "If you are scared, call that Reverend."

So, I say drink everything in moderation, *and* keep the Reverend's telephone number close by.

Couples, YOU CAN ACHIEVE NEWNESS AGAIN!

Thirty-seven

IS THERE A BULLY IN YOUR MARRIAGE?

A bully tries to make you do things that you don't want to do, and if you don't do them, then there are often consequences such as some form of abuse.

The marriage bully demands, "It is my way or the highway."

The marriage bully declares, "I control this marriage!" If that is the case, the marriage is on lockdown, and it can't grow.

You cannot be afraid of the marriage bully. You have to stand up for yourself.

When you recognize the marriage bully, it is time to confront the bully. It is time to negotiate. When you negotiate, the marriage wins.

Thirty-seven: Is There A Bully In Your Marriage?

Tip #37

•••

You must negotiate your do's and don'ts in your marriage if you wish to achieve newness again.

Couples, YOU CAN ACHIEVE NEWNESS AGAIN!

Thirty-eight

OVER ONE THOUSAND BENEFITS FOR JUST BEING MARRIED!

The Federal Defense of Marriage Act states there are 1,138 benefits for married people. Who/What else can give you this many benefits?

In addition to love and companionship, you can get social security benefits, health benefits, head-of-household status benefits, childcare credits, retirement benefits, death benefits and many more.

The Family and Medical Leave Act (FMLA) guarantees family and medical leave to employees to care for parents, children, or spouses.

Thirty-eight: Over One Thousand Benefits For Just Being Married!

Tip #38

• • •

Who wouldn't want to be married, with so many available benefits? I say, if Spring Fever has sprung, spring into marriage!

Couples, YOU CAN ACHIEVE NEWNESS AGAIN!

Thirty-nine
IN SICKNESS AND IN HEALTH

Do you remember that line when you took your marriage vows? You probably never thought seriously about the *sickness* part.

When your spouse becomes sick for an extended period, you must remember the vows you took.

You must be proactive on this one. This is not the time to walk out or act as if it does not involve you. You can't say it is his/her sickness. You must walk through it with your spouse for however long it takes, from a cold to cancer.

Tip #39

...

You commit to marriage from the birth of the marriage to the death of the marriage.

After Columbia Bible College And Seminary President Robertson McQuilkin's wife was diagnosed with Alzheimer's disease, he found himself torn between two commitments: One to his job and one to his wife.

He chose to quit his job to take care of his wife. He didn't just *say* his vows; he *lived* his vows, and he is quoted as saying, "If I take care of her another forty years, I'll still be in her debt." [Source: Christianity Today]

Couples, YOU CAN ACHIEVE NEWNESS AGAIN!

Forty

WILL PORNOGRAPHY ENHANCE OR DESTROY YOUR MARRIAGE?

Only the two spouses can answer this question.

There is a very fine line between what is permissible and pornography, and when you cross that line it is hard to recover.

Men are more prone to succumb to pornography than women are. This attraction usually starts during teenage years, but should stop at marriage.

William M. Struthers states that pornography affects the brain. It is like a drug. He says, "it is an image that you become focused on, which then, the chemical in your brain called dopamine is released, and before you know it, you are addicted." However, if you are focused on your spouse, there won't be a problem. (Porn is associated with social anxiety, depression, low motivation, erectile dysfunction, and distorted self-perceptions.)

Forty: Will Pornography Enhance Or Destroy Your Marriage?

Tip #40

•••

In marriage, pornography is a habit that must be broken unless both spouses are in complete agreement that it should continue.

Couples, YOU CAN ACHIEVE NEWNESS AGAIN!

Forty-one

HUSBANDS OFTEN SAY TO THEIR WIVES, "YOU ARE NOT MY MOTHER!"

A lot of people celebrate Mother's Day every second Sunday in May, but husbands sometimes get annoyed at their wives because their wives sometimes treat them as if they are children throughout their marriage, and not as the Man of the house. This is often played out by the tone of voice a wife uses when speaking to the husband - and it is not in a good way.

Many times, the husband has shouted to the wife scolding him about insufficient appreciation, "You are not my mother!"

However, this is seen both ways: Early in the marriage, the husband takes care of the wife as her dad probably did, so he becomes like the dad.

Later in the marriage, the wife takes care of her husband as a caring mother does for her children. Therefore, it is really not a bad thing unless the husband has been insulted to some degree by the wife in a way that

Forty-one: Husbands Often Say To Their Wives, "You Are Not My Mother!"

makes him feel emasculated. If this is the case, the husband is obligated to articulate his feelings to his wife, and the wife is obligated to listen.

The wife should never put the husband in a position to say "You are not my mother" because without realizing it, the wife is creating a negative tone of marriage that could result in behaviors you never imagined, nor want to experience.

Forty-one: Husbands Often Say To Their Wives, "You Are Not My Mother!"

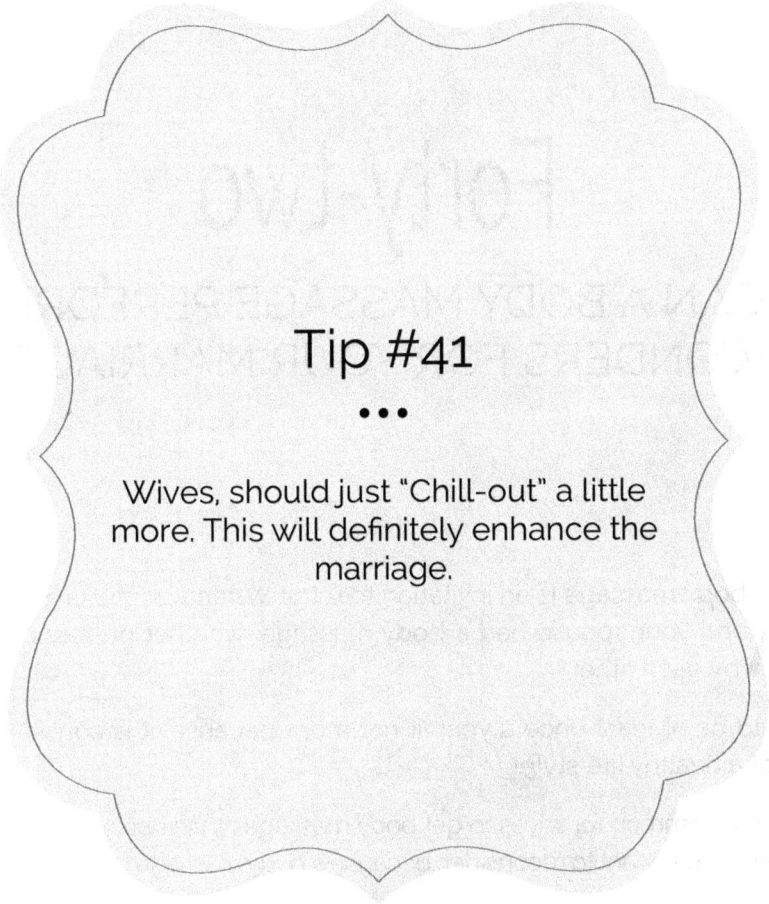

Tip #41

...

Wives, should just "Chill-out" a little more. This will definitely enhance the marriage.

Couples, YOU CAN ACHIEVE NEWNESS AGAIN!

Forty-two

CAN A BODY MASSAGE PERFORM WONDERS FOR YOUR MARRIAGE?

A body massage is an invitation to relax. When was the last time you and your spouse had a body massage, whether professionally or by each other?

It could be at least once a year, if not more because, it is considered as part of a healthy life style!

It is more common for wives to get body massages than husbands. However, husbands may want to reconsider, because a body massage does many good.

Why? Because a massage causes physiological changes in the body.

Such as:

1. **Relaxation Responses-** Your heart and breathing rate slow down, your blood pressure goes down, stress hormones decreases, and muscles relax.
2. **Mechanical Responses-** Increase in blood and lymph circulation, and relaxes the soft tissues such as muscles, tendons and ligaments.

[Source: American Massage Therapy Association; Expert Contributor: Beth Burgan]

Forty-two: Can A Body Massage Perform Wonders For Your Marriage?

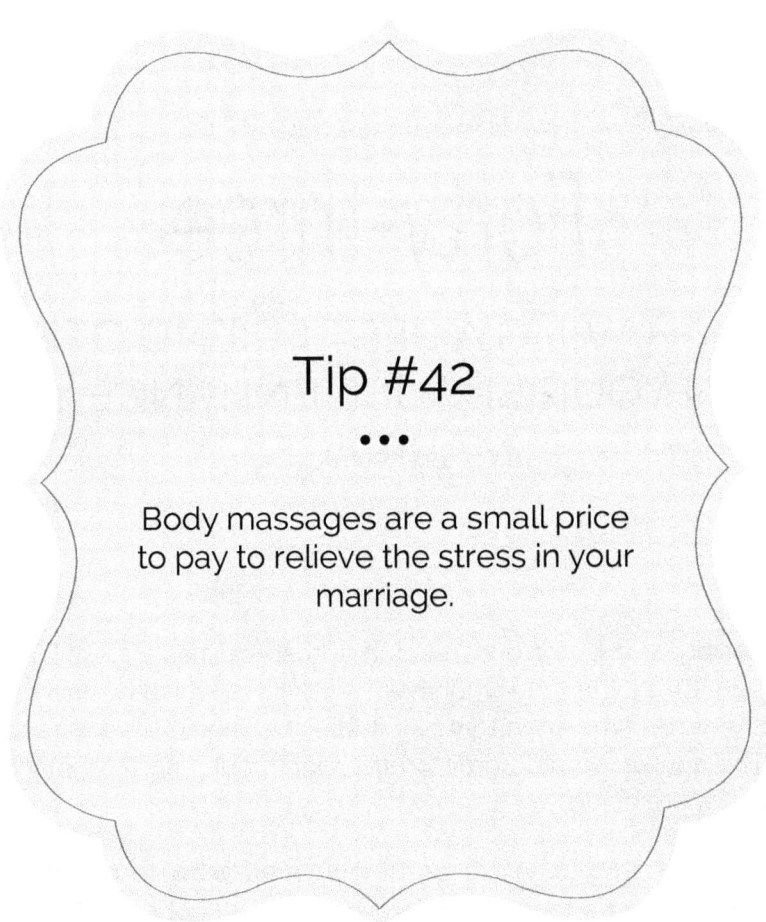

Tip #42

• • •

Body massages are a small price to pay to relieve the stress in your marriage.

Couples, YOU CAN ACHIEVE NEWNESS AGAIN!

Forty-three

CAN HAVING A BEST FRIEND OTHER THAN YOUR SPOUSE ENHANCE YOUR MARRIAGE?

Possibly! If it is not one-sided. If a husband has a best friend and spends a lot of time whenever he chooses, which takes away from the wife's time, then to make it fair, she should have a best friend also. The couple should agree on the nights out with their friends and where they are going.

It is not a bad thing to have a best friend at all because sometimes you may need someone to talk to. However, it should not cross the line with one spouse telling personal business about their marriage because this can actually harm a marriage.

Your best friend could either be your *mother, father, childhood friend, etc.,* However, when you are married, you should not divide too much of your time outside of your marital relationship especially if your best friend is not married.

Both spouses should agree if the best friend is good for your marriage.

Forty-three: Can Having A Best Friend Other Than Your Spouse Enhance Your Marriage?

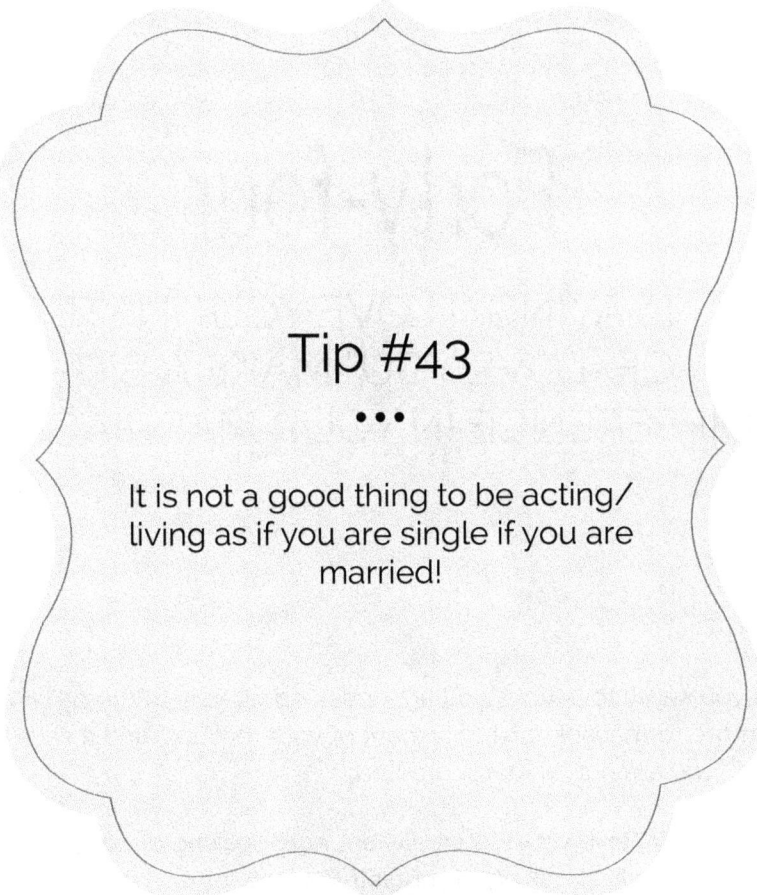

Tip #43

•••

It is not a good thing to be acting/living as if you are single if you are married!

Couples, YOU CAN ACHIEVE NEWNESS AGAIN!

Forty-four

CAN SAYING "I LOVE YOU" INSTEAD OF "LOVE YOU" MAKE A BIG DIFFERENCE IN YOUR MARRIAGE?

Yes and Yes!

When you say, "I love you," you are speaking directly to the other person. It is a more formal acknowledgement of your feelings; and it says to your spouse, "you are not taken for granted."

When you say, "love you," you really are not speaking directly to that person. You are really speaking to yourself. You are somewhat mumbling and it's more casual.

You must remember the excitement when you first told your spouse, (*probably* when you were dating), "I love you." However, later in marriage, the "I" just happens to drop off and now it is "Love You." Why?

Practice saying it again at least once a day and watch the wonders of love.

Forty-four: Can Saying "I Love You" Instead Of "Love You" Make a Big Different In Your Marriage?

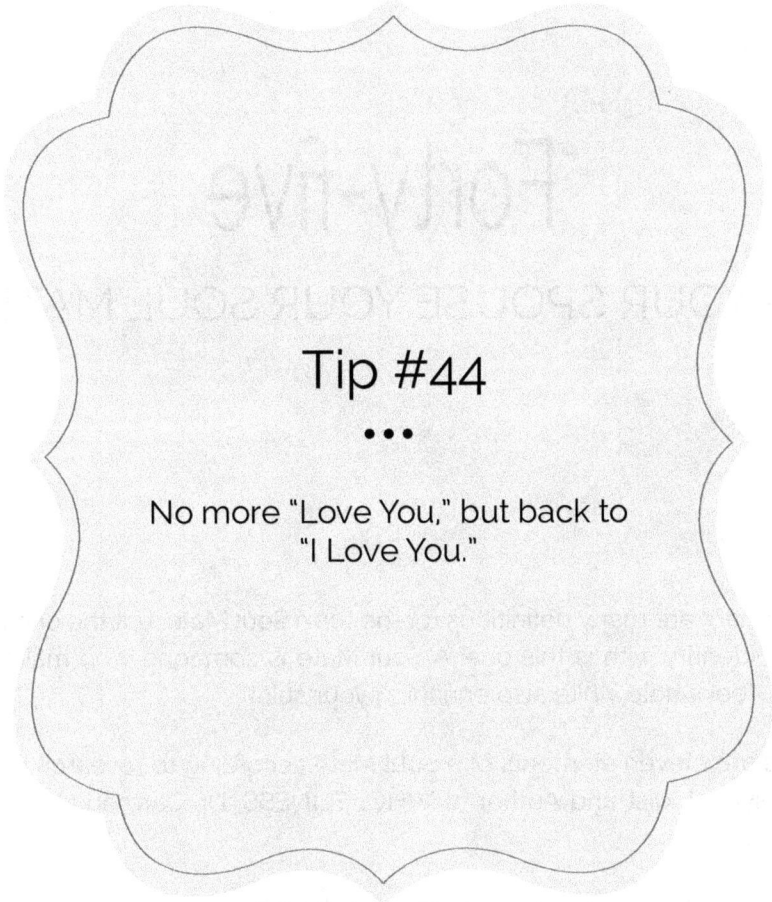

Tip #44

•••

No more "Love You," but back to "I Love You."

Couples, YOU CAN ACHIEVE NEWNESS AGAIN!

Forty-five
IS YOUR SPOUSE YOUR SOUL MATE?

There are many definitions for the term Soul Mate, but the one I most identify with is this one: A Soul Mate is someone who makes you feel whole while also enriching your spirit.

There are eleven elements of a Soul Mate according to research by Clinical Psychologist and Author of WHOLELINESS, Dr. Carmen Harra. Here are five of them:

1. You just have a feeling that you know he/she is the one.
2. It's the two of you against the world.
3. You look in each other's eyes, and not elsewhere, when talking to each other.
4. He or she was often, somehow, present in your past.
5. You just can't even imagine life without this person in your life.

Okay, so what's your answer?

Forty-five: Is Your Spouse Your Soul Mate?

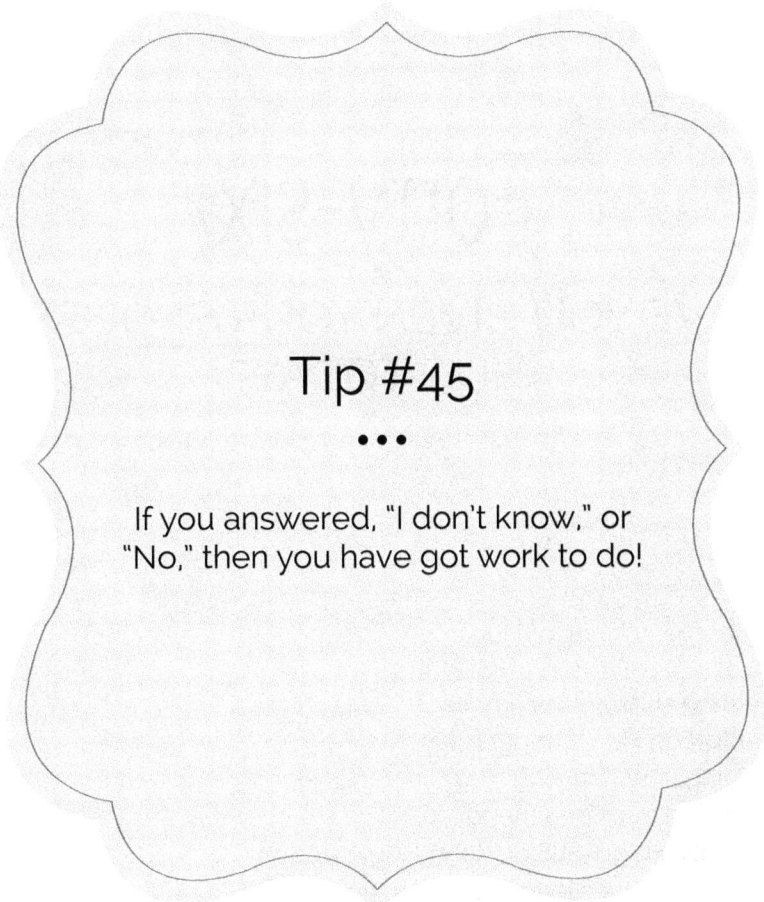

Tip #45

...

If you answered, "I don't know," or "No," then you have got work to do!

Couples, YOU CAN ACHIEVE NEWNESS AGAIN!

Forty-six
HAVE YOU GIVEN YOUR SPOUSE A HUG TODAY?

There are many kinds of Hugs:

1. Greeting Hug: Kiss on cheek
2. Comforting Hug: Longer hugs
3. Bonding Hug: Trusting Hug
4. Affection Hug: For a friend
5. Romantic Hug: Relation/long Hug/passion
6. Possession Hug: Jealousy/guarding property
7. Protection Hug: Puts arm around/safety
8. Domination Hug: A strong squeeze

Hugging seems so simple, yet, is so hard to do. According to Dr. Kenneth T. Whalum, Jr., Author of **Hip-Hop is Not Our Enemy**, (www.hiphopisnotourenemy.com), "Based on 30 years of clinical research and pastoral observation, hugging is uncomfortable for some because, hugging requires the complete and voluntary dropping of all "personal space" boundaries. You

Forty-six: Have You Given Your Spouse A Hug Today?

are required to let the other person get as close as humanly possible, which requires innate trust of the other person. If trust is an issue in the relationship, hugging doesn't come easy. For similar reasons, a guilty spouse finds it hard to be "open" enough to hug the person whose trust he/she has violated."

However, Hugging can work wonders. Husbands should initiate the hugs, especially if he's the kind of husband who hugs other women all day long, but never has the time to hug his own wife!

Family Therapist Virginia Satir, states people need four hugs a day for survival, eight hugs a day for maintenance, and twelve hugs a day for growth. That's twenty-four hugs a day, but she says a relationship can get along on at least eight per day. Ask your spouse if you can start with just one hug a day and build up to eight each day.

Forty-six: Have You Given Your Spouse A Hug Today?

Tip #46

•••

Hugs keep us alive!

Couples, YOU CAN ACHIEVE NEWNESS AGAIN!

Forty-seven

COULD EATING AT "HOOTERS" POSSIBLY ENHANCE YOUR MARRIAGE?

Many people have heard of Hooters where the service and **Hooter's World Famous Chicken wings are great!** They are a five-star restaurant chain and single men love to go there. Husbands love to go also, but often don't because the wife would rather eat at another restaurant where chicken wings are served.

Why? One of the reasons is those orange outfits worn by the waitresses. They definitely grab one's attention more than the chicken wings.

I believe, wives should reconsider and frequent the restaurant with their husbands, especially if they knew just how GREAT men often feel when they leave the restaurant.

Forty-seven: Could Eating at "Hooters" Possibly Enhance Your Marriage?

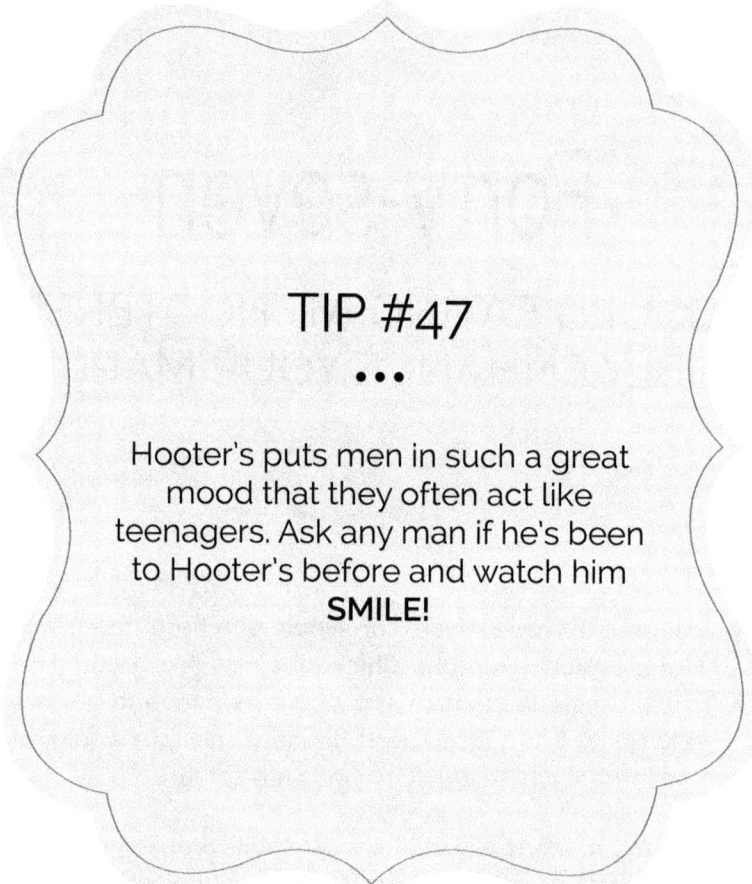

TIP #47

•••

Hooter's puts men in such a great mood that they often act like teenagers. Ask any man if he's been to Hooter's before and watch him **SMILE!**

Couples, YOU CAN ACHIEVE NEWNESS AGAIN!

Forty-eight

THE POLICY OF JOINT AGREEMENT WILL ENHANCE YOUR MARRIAGE

This document comes after the Marriage License to keep down conflicts within the Marriage. This is an effort to remember what you agreed on when it really comes to outside relationships including but not limited to family, friends, and associates.

The Policy of Joint Agreement is discussed in Dr. Willard F. Harley's book- *He Wins/She Wins, the Art of Marital Negotiations.*

1. It is a simply Written RULE that says:

"We, as a couple agree on these certain facts…" The balance of the policy is uniquely designed by each couple for their own marriage.

There should be at least three topics that you both agree on:

Forty-eight: The Policy of Joint Agreement

For example:

A. Don't lend money to relatives or friends without the other spouse knowing about it.
B. You can't allow a relative or friend to stay at your house for a month unless the two of you agree.
C. You don't just leave the house without telling your spouse where you are going and what time you may be back.

2. Then each of you sign it, frame it and hang it so that you can see it often.

Forty-eight: The Policy of Joint Agreement

Tip #48

• • •

Don't **hide** this policy like you've hidden your Marriage License.

Couples, YOU CAN ACHIEVE NEWNESS AGAIN!

Forty-nine

TO ENHANCE YOUR MARRIAGE OR RELATIONSHIP
STOP
DOMESTIC VIOLENCE

According to Christina Coleman, in **Global Grind Magazine,** 85% of domestic violence victims are Women. That shows a whole lot of abuse going on.

In the State of Tennessee, for a two-year period (2011-2013), The Tennessee Bureau of Investigation (TBI) indicates that 247,000 cases of domestic or intimate partner violence were reported.

Domestic Violence is often the result of jealousy and rejection. Domestic Violence Should NOT be a part of marriage, or any other kind of relationship. It is not love, but HATE. When it occurs, it often leads to PRISON or DEATH.

The first time something happens out of the ordinary, in the name of love, it is time to communicate with a third party. Listed are a few resources: Pastor, close friend, parent, family member, teacher and:

YWCA of Greater Memphis
The Healing Word Counseling Center of Memphis
Sophia's House of Memphis
National Coalition Against Domestic Violence

Forty-nine: To Enhance Your Marriage or Relationship

Tip #49

•••

Marriage or any relationship should not include Domestic Violence!

Couples, YOU CAN ACHIEVE NEWNESS AGAIN!

Final Chapter (50)
WHY L O V E DOESN'T LAST

~Too Many Distractions~

Because too much is going on in that relationship

One night while at home in bed, I was "channel surfing," (as we all do), and I came across the movie *"Gone with the Wind."* For some reason, I decided to stay on that channel and watch this famous 1939 movie. You may remember it. The two main characters in the movie are Scarlett O'Hara, played by Vivien Leigh; and Rhett Butler, played by Clark Gable.

It's a love-hate "love story" between the two. In addition, Scarlett had emotional problems and lastly, her love for Rhett came just a little too late. Scarlett and Rhett dated for a while then they got married. They had a good life, so it seemed. They had it all. They had the looks: He was *fine*, and she was pretty. They had a beautiful house, money, and all the trappings of wealth. You name it they had it, but Scarlett was in love with somebody

Final Chapter (50): Why L O V E doesn't last

else. Haven't you heard the song by R&B singer Jasmine Sullivan that says, "I am in love with someone else?"

Scarlett is in love with a guy named Ashley Wilkes who is about to marry another woman – Melanie – who happens to be Scarlett's best friend. Though Scarlett tells Ashley that she is in love with him, he still chooses to marry Melanie, who he says would make him a better wife. Well, since Melanie marries Ashley, Scarlett goes ahead and marries Rhett, though she didn't love him. Throughout the marriage, they fight like cats and dogs (as my Mother Margaret would say!)

As time went on, her husband Rhett continued to try to please her, but it wasn't enough. She still wanted her best friend's husband. When her friend Melanie became ill, she and her husband went over to their house. Melanie died and she tried to comfort her friend's husband; the man that she truly loved. She told him that now that your wife has died we could be together, all the while Scarlett's husband, Rhett was watching and listening.

The man she loved turned her down. When she realized that he didn't love her after all, she decided she needed to play her cards right. She looked around for her husband and realized that he was gone. Rhett had tipped out when he saw how his wife was acting over this other man. Rhett finally realized that the woman, whom he tried to love repeatedly, didn't love him.

When Scarlett finally made it home, she saw that Rhett was packing and about to be out. She then proceeds to tell him, "I really do love you, and give me another chance," but Rhett, realizing that he had done all that he could do to get this woman to love him, delivers one of the most memorable lines in movie history: *"Frankly, my dear, I don't give a damn!"* Then he did something that could happen in your marriage if you don't find a way to keep love alive: He walked out the door, never to return. Rhett Butler was **Gone with the Wind.**

Wind can represent many things, but for our purposes, wind means a current of air carrying an odor, scent, or sound. Scarlett was blown and tossed by the wind. She was carrying a scent and it was not a sweet smelling scent, though she wore the finest perfume. She wanted a married man! She also carried a sound that was painful to hear. Apparently, she did not

Final Chapter (50): Why L O V E doesn't last

know about the biblical book of James, where it says, *"Consider it pure joy, my brothers, whenever you face trials of many kinds, because you know that the testing of your faith develops perseverance. Perseverance must finish its work so that you may be mature and complete, not lacking anything. If any of you lacks wisdom, he should ask God, who gives generously to all without finding fault, and it will be given to him.*

But when he asks, he must believe and not doubt, because he who doubts is like a wave of the sea, blown and tossed by the wind. That man should not think he will receive anything from the Lord; he is a double-minded man, unstable in all he does." (James 1:2-8)

This text instructs us to consider it pure joy when we face trials of many kinds, but not when we bring them upon ourselves. Scarlett knew that Ashley was married, and so was she. The text goes on to say, let perseverance finish its work so that you may be mature and complete, not lacking anything. In other words in spite of difficulties, obstacles, discouragement, keep trying to reach your goal. However, Scarlett was in the wrong, so she was making it impossible to reach her goal.

Right after it says, "Lacking anything," verse five gets specific. It says, "If any of you lack wisdom, you should ask God, who gives generously to all without finding fault, and it will be given unto you." Well, what exactly is wisdom? It is the ability to discern or judge what is true, right, or lasting. It is insight into something. Why would James be specific here? It is because many people think that their lives are their own and they can do what they want to do. Scarlett wanted to do it her way, and it brought her heartache. She not only lost one man, but two men.

I remember when I almost didn't use wisdom, and it would have changed the course of history for my life. When I met Dr. Kenneth T. Whalum, Jr., he wanted me, but I was dating another guy. I thought I couldn't live without that man. Everyone - but me - could see that the other guy was not the one for me, but I was in love. No matter how nice Kenneth was, I was not using God's wisdom. I remember writing Kenneth a "Dear John" letter, telling him he was the nicest guy, but I was going to stay with my boyfriend. Guess what? For some reason I never mailed the letter. I remember praying to God. "God, Kenneth will be coming home from law school in May.

Final Chapter (50): Why L O V E doesn't last

Please show me what to do. I can't have these two boyfriends any longer, since he will be back in Memphis for good."

The scripture says, if you lack wisdom, you should ask God who gives generously to all without finding fault, and it will be given to you. I asked God for wisdom and the rest is history. Thirty-two years later, I'm still happily married to Kenneth.

You see, sometimes we just don't know what is good for us, but if you are on God's side, He will show up just in time. The text goes on to say, "but when you ask, you must believe and not doubt, because the one who doubts is like a wave of the sea, blown and tossed by the wind. Those who doubt should not think they should receive anything from the Lord; they are double-minded and unstable in all they do. Therefore, as I expound more on Wind or "Gone with the Wind" this phrase means doubters, those who don't believe God's word. Those who don't study to show themselves approved. Those who are constantly blown and tossed by wind. And, those who are unstable in everything they do.

Just like Scarlett who ended up with a broken heart because she was double-minded, God says those who doubt should not think they would receive anything from the Lord. Scarlett could never get it together because her heart had been broken and never made whole. Until you ask God to fix your broken heart from whatever relationship that hurt you, it will continue to manifest itself. Whether it was a husband, wife, sister, brother, aunt, friend, stepfather, or stepmother, and whether it was yesterday, last year or many years ago, only when you ask God to fix it and make it whole will your complete healing manifest in every area of your life.

A healthy heart is a heart that loves everybody. When a heart is broken, it picks and chooses who it wants to love. That's why you can treat this person mean and treat that person nice. You are not using wisdom when you do not ask God to fix your broken heart, so you go through life in pieces, never quite getting where you want to be. In actuality, you doubt God, and what He can do for you, and therefore you are tossed about as the wind going here and there. As God looks at you trying to do life yourself, He says, "Go ahead. Don't expect my blessings because you are double-minded. You have your own wisdom."

Final Chapter (50): Why L O V E doesn't last

He says, "If you had my wisdom, you would be born again. I have tried and tried to help you. I have given you so many opportunities and so much time. Yet you are still playing me for a fool! You continue doing what you want. You don't even give me seven hours a week; not even one hour per day." You really think you have time, but just when you think you have one more chance to get it right with me, the LORD just might say to you, "**Frankly, My Dear, I Don't Give A Damn!**" (Meaning *damnation* in the biblical sense.)

In conclusion, love doesn't last because too often we let people separate us from the love of God, which is the only love that really matters. God's love is the only love that stands at the end of the day. Romans 8:39 says, "*What can separate us from the love of God?*" I say, "A *man* can (if you let him!)" R&B singer Chante Moore released a hit song in 2014 that includes the following lyrics, which I suggest you adopt as your own:

I've been waiting all my life for that someone who will truly satisfy. I thought that if he came, he would make everything all right. I was looking for a friend, looking for a man, I was longing for flesh and more, suddenly one moment I knew, Jesus I want you, to touch me with your spirit; Jesus I need you to hide me under your wings, more than anyone on earth, more than anyone on earth, more than anything on earth, Jesus I want YOU!

Final Chapter (50): Why L O V E doesn't last

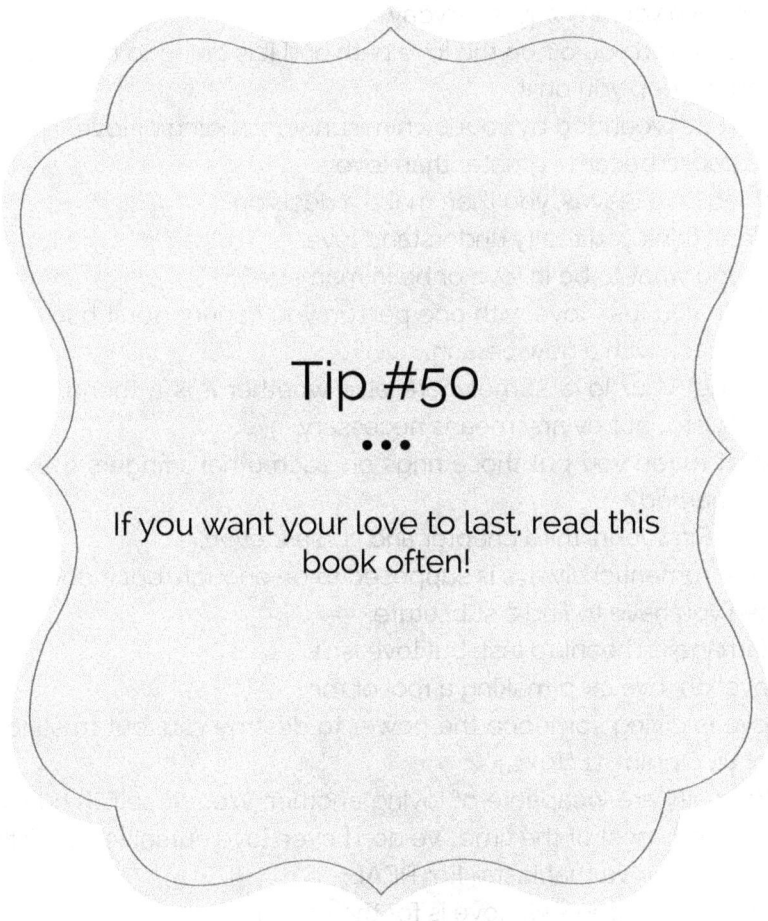

Tip #50

...

If you want your love to last, read this book often!

Couples, YOU CAN ACHIEVE NEWNESS AGAIN!

WISDOM FROM SHEILA WHALUM AND OTHERS

1. You can't make love when you are no longer in love.
2. I will love you anyway, everyday.
3. Lust started you off on the love path and it is going to take the love of God to keep you on it.
4. Don't be wounded by your own misunderstanding of love.
5. His cause became greater than love.
6. When love leaves, you then make a decision.
7. I don't think you really understand love.
8. Do you want to be in love or be in marriage?
9. When you lose love with one person you cannot get it back: you get love back with a new person.
10. You get your love somewhere else whether it is a friend, shopping, book, etc., but by any means necessary.
11. What made you put those rings on each other's fingers the day you got married?
12. Love-First John, third chapter and verse eleven.
13. Love (romantic) always is supposed to be enough, but it does not last; then you have to find a substitute.
14. Marriage is meant to last, but love isn't.
15. Love, oh love stop making a fool of me.
16. Love is giving someone the power to destroy you, but trusting them not to. Oprah- 11/10/13
17. We really are incapable of loving another. We are selfish human beings. And, most of the time, we don't even love ourselves. Christ's love is the only love that lasts- For REAL!
18. I heard someone say, "love is for the young."
19. Marriage is all about a man finding his ambition so that he can give his wife all that she needs in place of love.
20. A man and a woman are human. Somebody is going to mess up which tampers with the love.
21. The pain won't go away: Whatever happened, even as a child, it keeps coming up so love doesn't last because the pain won't go away.
22. I Blame You by Ledisi.

23. The marriage broke down because somebody stopped loving.
24. Which (B) do men love the best?
25. Some Men love the Booty, the Breast, Beauty, and the Bible: In that order.
26. Do you have to have love in your marriage? Yes, according to the word of God.
27. Broken love-you can fall in love many times with different people but when the one you love breaks your heart, you can't get it back. It's gone.
28. What's love got to do with marriage? Absolutely nothing! You need a helpmeet.
29. Love never felt so good- Michael Jackson and Justin Timberlake (But, love doesn't last)
30. Does helpmeet really mean love?
31. I am in love with myself.
32. When it happens the first time, love is gone. This line from The Jackie Robinson movie captures this, "When he took his eyes off me, it was over." At one point in time, they loved each other.
33. Did you fool around and fall in love?
34. When you are head over hills in love, you will get hurt, so stop at the hill.
35. When you love somebody, you ooh and awe! When was the last time you ooh'ed and awe'd about your spouse?
36. There is bitter love, business love, even "real" love, but not romantic love in marriage because it leaves early. It was just lust before marriage.
37. Enjoy the ride for a short time.
38. Love doesn't last because you abused me
39. Love is a passionate kiss.
40. He that findeth a wife, findeth a good thing? Proverbs 18:22
41. 1 Chronicles, chapter 16 verse 34: "O give thanks to the Lord, for he is good; his steadfast love endures forever.
42. Marriage is a beautiful thing when it is right and you have to get it right: It is not the wedding.
43. I keep on falling in and out of love with you by Alicia Keys
44. It's cheaper to keep her by B.B. King
45. The Wedding; then the distractions.

46. I choose me. I got to go with me by Tamia
47. What I do love about weddings is reading the announcements in the New York Times. Joan Rivers
48. Once in a while, right in the middle of an ordinary life, love gives us a fairy tale.
49. To enhance your marriage stop the domestic violence
50. Say to yourself- "I love ME!"

EPILOGUE

BY
DR. DEE LOFTON, DM

You've heard it all before. Those reasons why a love that lasts is so wonderful; how you can change yourself to be more loveable, or change him/her so *they* are more loveable. YET, here we are, still wondering why love does not last. Love is, so not a cartoon, so not a love song (though we find comfort in our music), so not simple. When asked how do you define love, what immediately comes to your mind?

While the definitions are far from cookie cutter, each of us probably has it at least half-right. Going back to one of the greatest philosophers of our time, we find insight into the kinds of love humans practice, and why some types of love 'fit' better than others.

Aristotle *(Nicomachean Ethics)* describes love as an emotion practiced in friendships of *utility* (shallow and easily dissolved), *pleasure* (based on passion, satisfaction), and *virtue* (long lasting, resilient). The greatest of these is the love found in a virtuous friendship. Why? Because it incorporates all of the elements of a symbiotic love, yet depends upon the self-maturity of the partners to survive, in good times and bad, happy and sad. Hey, if you are looking for a love that will last forever, and you haven't added *Let's Stay Together* (Al Green) to your love playlist, maybe you should.

Taking into consideration your personal history when it comes to love, what do you see in your love future? Look for love in all the right places, starting with inside of you.

UNBREAK YOUR HEART!

Staying in a relationship where your time is spent trying to 'figure out' the other person can only lead to heartbreak and disappointment. Mature

Epilogue

Love finds its own path, beyond feelings *about* someone else, toward understanding what *you* feel, what *you* need from the relationship. Secondary Feelings (like anger, disappointment, frustration, and rage) keep you on the defensive, unable to fully accept or give real love. Secondary Feelings are comfortable and may feel safe, particularly when defensive response patterns are learned behaviors from childhood, or strongly observed (seen as working) in our adult relationships.

Primary Feelings are feelings like hurt, sadness, fear, anxiety, hopelessness, and helplessness. Primary Feelings make us vulnerable, and are not easily expressed. These feelings open the door to mature love, exceed pleasure and lust, and therefore, are scary and not trusted.

What is your relationship by-product? When the relationship ends, what are you leaving behind? Do you walk away saying, 'I got what I needed from him/her, no harm no foul?' Know that there is always a carbon footprint left behind when even the simplest friendships end. Our goal is to recall, what went right, what went wrong, what pleased and what displeased us during the relationship. If you carry-forward old news into the next relationship, chances are it will end the same way as the last, hurt worse, and take longer to move on.

DON'T BE STUCK IN THE MUD

No matter how much you love another person, there is no way around the work, if you want a successful relationship with another human being. Even pets require something from you before they can show and receive love. Move beyond friendships based on gain, or simple pleasure, find someone *worthy* of engaging in your Primary Feelings and the subsequent feelings of vulnerability. Allow your partner to be in relationship WITH you, build upon symbiotic beginnings, and enjoy real friendship, respect, joy, and true interest in the other person and self. When partners get stuck in Secondary Feelings (like resentment), that romantic love from a "friend" may begin to look and feel more like sleeping with the enemy, and be the death knell of love.

We all want a complete love, where the bad days don't ruin the good days, where we are safe feeling out of sorts and needing alone time. Be a friend for yourself. Give *you* all of the encouragement, respect, trust, and honor you would offer someone else you considered a good friend. Montaigne, a 14th century essayist puts it this way, "the love I speak of has no seams, knows no bounds, exists within and outside of me, and when shared, is like my soul has merged with another, blending so completely."

Who wouldn't want a love like that? When given freely and accepted completely, conforming to a simple, mild symbiotic friendship is no longer possible.

DISCOVER YOUR MUTUAL BENEFIT

Self-examination is a powerful tool in relationships. Not dwelling on your faults, weaknesses, or thoughtless indiscretions, but asking the hard questions. Why are you in this relationship? Are you getting what you need, while giving back in a loving way to your partner? Maturity in love is what makes love last. Aristotle refers to the strongest type of relationship as a "virtuous friendship," a "most glorious attainment" achieved by the very few. Why is this level of friendship so rare? Because achieving virtue, on any level, is hard work. First, you must be a person of virtue (trustworthy and honest), and you must require the same virtues from your mate/partner. Secondly, your circle of trust, by nature, must be very small for the level of commitment required; spreading your love is not an option. Thirdly, the person to whom you offer a virtuous friendship must be prized and loved freely, as a by-product of shared virtue.

MAKE THE SHIFT TO AN INTIMATE CONNECTION

In *The Spell of Symbiosis* (Fenaroli, 2010) discusses the attributes of a symbiotic love, and why this type of love "feels" like the real thing and is so desirable to have in your life. Symbiotic love is based on mutual benefit and desire, discovering what we can do to make each other happy. The down side is there is often very little discussion on how to handle the relationship when one or the other fails to deliver on these inferred promises. Even in grade school, children fall out of like with each other because of disappointment (you picked him for your team and not me) or some unintended infraction (you didn't ask me to have lunch with you today). This

Epilogue

pattern even emerges in adult relationships, particularly those based on actions.

Now you know, having read Sheila Whalum's *"Why Love Doesn't Last"* all of the ways we can sabotage relationships and destroy the love we had. Make the shift from *what love can do for me*, to *what I can do for YOUR love*. This love commitment takes time, and a desire to have, and to give love. Hence, this type of love should be rare, offered in only the best relationship - one already based on friendship, pleasure, mutual benefit, desire, and intimacy. To achieve this, one or both partners have to deepen their perspective and journey into Primary Feelings. This introspection requires risking the possibility that a mature love can be found and enjoyed by both parties.

Hope for the Love Dream Team, one that is symbiotic, intimate, and virtuous. Allow for an Intimate Connection *[in your most desirable relationships!]* and recognize that a relationship is between two different people, with different life experiences, beliefs, and values. The Love Dream Team is the greatest of all loves because it can be enjoyed for its own sake, it reaches beyond mere like and lust, and it brings with it the opportunity for a love, that will last.

Are you looking for love? Go on, findeth your good thing; and then, make it last, forever.

BIBLIOGRAPHY

Aristotle. *Nicomachean Ethics*. Trans. Joe Sachs. Newburyport, MA: Focus Publishing

Fenaroli, C. (2010). The spell of symbiosis in couples relationships. http://www.acoupleatatime.com/the-spell-of-symbiosis-in-couples-relationships.html

Moore, C. (2013). Moore is More. *Jesus, I Want You*. Newton, NJ: Shanachie Records

Wendyo. (2011). Life on the L-Edge. http://open.salon.com/blog/wendyo/2011/08/02/on_symbiosis_-_-_for_we_who_love_that_way

RESOURCES FOR C.A.N.A. BOOK CLUB

2003
The Successful Family by Dr. Creflo & Taffi Dollar

2004
An Outrageous Commitment by Dr. Ronn Elmore

2005
Smart Couples Finish Rich by David Bach

2006
Love & Respect by Emerson Eggerichs

2007
Your Best Life Now by Joel Osteen

2008
The Five Love Languages by Gary Chapman

2009
Managing Your Emotions by Joyce Meyer

2010
Reposition Yourself by T.D. Jakes

2011
The Power of Prayer to Change Your Marriage by Stormie Omartian

2012
Love and War by John & Stasi Eldredge

2013
A Unified Theory of Happiness by Andrea F. Polard

2014
He Wins, She Wins
Learning the Art of Martial Negotiation by Willard F. Harley, Jr.

*The years represent the year that CANA studied that particular book. And, many of the sources are from the Worldwide Web/Internet

ABOUT THE AUTHOR

Sheila Whalum is the Wife and First Lady of Dr. Kenneth T. Whalum, Jr., Pastor of *The New Olivet Baptist Church*, in Memphis, Tennessee. Dr. Whalum is a member of the Memphis and Shelby County Schools Board of Education and Author of *Hip-Hop Is Not Our Enemy*. They have been married for 32 years. Sheila is the mother of three talented sons: Saxophonist, Kenneth T. Whalum III (Crystal), Singer, Kortland Kirk Whalum and Trombonist, Kameron Timothy Whalum. She is granny to Kenneth T. Whalum IV.

She is President of Olivet Baptist Credit Union, and President of Aliehs, Inc., (O'Sheilas Beauty and Barber Shop and Christ-Like Modeling). She retired from City of Memphis Government as the Deputy Director of Finance. Sheila is a graduate of Leadership Memphis. She has a Master of Business Administration from the University of Phoenix, a Bachelor of Arts Degree in Communications with a minor in English from the University of Memphis. She received a certificate from Rhodes College for the Institute for Executive Leadership. She is a product of Memphis City Schools, where she was elected Queen of her High School "Miss Carver of 1978."

She is a Mentor at the University of Memphis Fogelman Business College, MILE (Memphis Institute of Leadership Education) Program; She is 2nd Vice- Chair for the Girl Scouts/Heart of the South; Community Advisory Board Member for Baptist Women's Hospital; Past GPN (Going Places Network) Consultant for Dress for Success/Walmart; Co-Founder of BAMM (Bust-A-Move-Monday) for small businesses and is deeply involved in her church - The New Olivet Baptist Church - www.olivetbc.com.

She is past liaison for the City of Memphis on the Memphis/Shelby County Airport Authority Board. She served as committee member for the City of Memphis Hardship Deferred Compensation Plan, the Retirement System Investment Committee, and the Operating Cash Committee. She is past board member for "Friends for Life Aids Awareness Program."

About The Author

She regularly participates as a runner in the St. Jude Half Marathon (13.1 miles).

Sheila's previous books: *Destined to be a Preacher's Wife* (2001), *Pretty Woman Too: The Truth About Jealousy* (2007), and *The Stimulus Package: Why Men Cheat* (2011). To order, visit www.sheilawhalum.com, or call the New Olivet at 901-454-7777.

Favorite Scripture:

Psalm 37, "Fret not thyself because of evil doers for they shall soon be cut down like the grass and withered away. Trust in the Lord and do good and He will give you the desires of your heart."

Join me, and Dr. Whalum, along with the CANA Facilitators every Sunday at 9:30am until 10:30am for one hour of Marriage Talk only at The New Olivet Baptist Church, 3084 Southern Avenue, Memphis, Tennessee 38111, 901-454-7777.

I am Sheila Whalum.

Connect with me on Facebook (Sheila Whalum), Twitter @sheilawhalum, Instagram or email at sheilawhalum@comcast.net, and let's talk about it some more. www.sheilawhalum.com

www.ingramcontent.com/pod-product-compliance
Lightning Source LLC
Chambersburg PA
CBHW050642160426
43194CB00010B/1777